PLANS
PURPOSES
& PURSUITS

Kenneth E. Hagin

Unless otherwise indicated, all Scripture quotations in this volume are from the *King James Version* of the Bible.

Second Printing 1988

ISBN 0-89276-512-7

In the U.S. write:
Kenneth Hagin Ministries
P.O. Box 50126
Tulsa, OK 74150-0126

In Canada write:
Kenneth Hagin Ministrie
P.O. Box 335
Islington (Toronto), Ontar
Canada, M9A 4X3

The Gifts and Calling of God
Signs of the Times
Learning To Flow With the Spirit of God
The Glory of God
Hear and Be Healed
*New Thresholds of Faith
*Prevailing Prayer to Peace
Concerning Spiritual Gifts
Bible Faith Study Course
Bible Prayer Study Course
The Holy Spirit and His Gifts
*The Ministry Gifts (Study Guide)
Seven Things You Should Know About Divine Healing
El Shaddai
Zoe: The God-Kind of Life
A Commonsense Guide to Fasting
Must Christians Suffer?
The Woman Question
The Believer's Authority
Ministering to Your Family
How You Can Be Led by the Spirit of God
What To Do When Faith Seems Weak and Victory Lost
The Name of Jesus
Growing Up, Spiritually
Bodily Healing and the Atonement
Exceedingly Growing Faith
Understanding the Anointing
I Believe in Visions
Understanding How To Fight the Good Fight of Faith
The Art of Intercession
Plans, Purposes, and Pursuits

BOOKS BY KENNETH HAGIN JR.

*Man's Impossibility — God's Possibility
Because of Jesus
The Key to the Supernatural
*Faith Worketh by Love
Blueprint for Building Strong Faith
*Seven Hindrances to Healing
*The Past Tense of God's Word
Healing: A Forever-Settled Subject
How To Make the Dream God Gave You Come True
Faith Takes Back What the Devil's Stolen
"The Prison Door Is Open — What Are You Still Doing Inside?"
Itching Ears
Where Do We Go From Here?
How To Be a Success in Life
Get Acquainted With God
Showdown With the Devil
Unforgiveness
The Answer for Oppression
Is Your Miracle Passing You By?
Commanding Power
The Life of Obedience
Ministering to the Brokenhearted

*These titles are also available in Spanish. Information about other foreign translations of several of the above titles (i.e., Dutch, Finnish, French, German, Indonesian, Polish, Russian, Swahili, and Swedish) may be obtained by writing to: Kenneth Hagin Ministries, P.O. Box 50126, Tulsa, Oklahoma 74150-0126.

Contents

Acknowledgment

Acknowledgment

A special thanks to Miss Angela Crews, administrative assistant for Lynette and me, for the final editing of this book. Working with a very tight deadline, Angela took a manuscript edited by Billye Brim, a portion of a manuscript edited by Kimberly Hjelt, and hundreds of pages of notes and sermon tape transcripts to compile the copy for this book, *Plans, Purposes, and Pursuits*. I know you will agree that the message of this book which Angela so beautifully put together is so vital to the Church today.

Kenneth Hagin Jr

Chapter 1
Visitation

Not as though I had already attained, either were already perfect [mature or full grown]: but I follow after, if that I may apprehend that for which also I am apprehended of Christ Jesus.

Brethren, I count not myself to have apprehended: but this one thing I do, forgetting those things which are behind, and reaching forth unto those things which are before,

I press toward the mark for the prize of the high calling of God in Christ Jesus.

— Philippians 3:12-14

And I, brethren, when I came to you, came not with excellency of speech or of wisdom, declaring unto you the testimony of God.

For I determined not to know any thing among you, save Jesus Christ, and him crucified.

And I was with you in weakness, and in fear, and in much trembling.

And my speech and my preaching was not with enticing words of man's wisdom, but in demonstration of the Spirit and of power:

That your faith should not stand in the wisdom of men, but in the power of God.

— 1 Corinthians 2:1-5

Several days before our annual Campmeeting in 1987, I had a visitation from the Lord. As I relate that visitation, I share it with you in weakness and in reverence and

1

in much trembling because of the awesomeness of God's power and His Presence. Paul said, *"I was with you in weakness, and in fear ... "* (1 Cor. 2:3). Of course, that didn't mean he was afraid like you would be afraid of a rattlesnake or a tornado. Paul meant that he had a godly fear, an awe, and a reverence for God. It is with that same reverence that I now relate to you that awesome visitation I had from the Lord the week before our Campmeeting.

First, let me explain that I do most of my praying at night. Most of my life I have been a night person. I'm older now and have changed some, but I have always been more alert at midnight than at any other hour of the day. That is why I used to do all of my studying at night. Many times I have studied and read all night long.

I got in the habit of praying during the night when I was bedfast in 1933 and 1934. I couldn't pray any other way except in bed, because I was bedfast — tied to that bed. I couldn't get up and walk. I remember one night in particular, I prayed all night long. I never slept at all; I just prayed. Several nights I prayed nearly all night long. Many nights I would pray an hour or two before I went to sleep.

I always looked forward to nighttime when everyone else was in bed and things got quiet, so that I could pray. In the daytime, someone always had to sit in the room with me. That went on for many months because they thought I was going at any moment, so they would only allow one person in the room at a time and that person had to sit with me. I got into the habit of praying at night when I could be alone, and I guess I have just followed that through the years. Many times, God has spoken to me in the night.

On July 16, the Thursday morning preceding our annual Campmeeting, I was awakened and I couldn't get back to sleep, so I began to pray in the Spirit. As I prayed in the Spirit in other tongues, I kept saying these words over in English: *"Plans, purposes."* Plans and purposes. I said to the Lord, "Lord, that is not all of that. I know it isn't," and I kept on praying in tongues. Finally, I prayed out in English, *"Plans, purposes, and pursuits."* Plans, purposes, and pursuits!

I was caught up into the Spirit and I began to see and understand man's plans as they related to God's plans. I could see that many times men had plans that were good and even thoroughly scriptural. But they were not *God's* plans.

This experience was unusual and it lasted almost three hours. Part of it was revelation, and part of it was a vision. It began about three o'clock in the morning, and the last time I looked at the clock, it was almost six o'clock.

When I was caught up into the Spirit to where Jesus was standing, it seemed that Jesus and I were standing up a little higher than the ceiling of the Tulsa Convention Center, looking down on our Campmeeting services which were scheduled to begin there the following Monday. I saw the Monday night service unfold before us, and I saw many things that would happen in the other services throughout the week. Jesus was the narrator and He explained what was taking place as I looked on.

As I stood there with Jesus — Jesus narrating and explaining the things that were happening in the services — I saw that this Campmeeting would be one of the most monumental and momentous Campmeetings we have ever had. I saw that the results of this Campmeeting would be forthcoming for a long, long time.

As I was standing up there with Jesus seeing all this unfold, I asked Him, "Lord, why didn't You visit me far enough in advance so we could have advertised to the people that this Campmeeting was going to be unusual? More people would have come if they would have known that."

Jesus answered, "The reason I didn't was because then the curiosity seekers and those seeking the sensational would have come. I just wanted those people to be here that I had directed to come."

Sad to say, in the Body of Christ there are those people who are just seeking the sensational. They are always seeking after anything that is new. Those people would have come with the wrong *purpose*. They would be the ones to say, "Let's go hear Brother Hagin! He's had another visitation! Let's go hear about it!" They are also usually the ones who take what you say and twist it.

Some people pick up on one part of what you say, twist it, and go off into excess and error and create confusion in the Body of Christ. There will probably be those who will read this book and take what I am saying out of context and get off into error. However, misguided people prone to error *should not* keep us from flowing with what is Biblical and right. It should *not* keep us from flowing with what the Holy Spirit is wanting to teach the Body of Christ in this hour! I believe that those who have ears to hear will hear what the Spirit is saying to the Church in this hour and will cooperate with Him to help usher in the move of God all of our hearts so earnestly desire.

A New Beginning

Only two or three times in the many years of my ministry have I had an experience like this one which took place prior to Campmeeting '87. The first such experience I had occurred in 1953.

I was praying in the Spirit on a Friday night and I saw my Sunday night service. When it came time for the service Sunday night, I just acted out what I had seen myself do. Marvelous, miraculous things happened in that service.

Then I had another experience like that in 1954 when I was preaching in California at a convention for a Full Gospel denomination. I had gotten off to sleep one night, but I woke up in the night with a sense of urgency to pray. I lay there praying quietly in the Spirit, not disturbing anyone, until about four o'clock in the morning. All of a sudden, I saw my service that night. Among other things, I saw a woman who had been brought in on a stretcher get up in front of everyone and walk off healed. When it came time for my service, I just acted out what I had seen myself do, and everything happened just as I had seen it! A woman was carried into the service on a stretcher, and she got up and walked off healed!

In the 1987 visitation with the Lord, Jesus told me some things that He is wanting to do in this day in the Church — *His plans* — and why He has not been able to do them. If the Body of Christ will cooperate with God, and get in line with His *plan* and His *purposes,* and *pursue* that plan, then God will be able to accomplish what *He* wants to in this day!

The Body of Christ has been in the shallow water of a new beginning for the last two or three years. We are just now moving out into another new beginning. We are just getting to the place where the Lord can begin to do some of the things He has wanted to do in this day and in this hour!

The things Jesus explained to me in this visitation were to help get the Body of Christ ready for this next great move of God's Spirit upon the earth. The spiritual truths that Jesus shared in this visitation are just simply the springboard, so to speak, which will spring the Body of Christ into a realm of the supernatural in a way and in a place that we have barely been before. Why? Because we will be following His *plans* and His *purposes* and *pursuing* them!

In the wave of God's blessing that is coming upon the earth, the things that have been manifested occasionally will become commonplace with the Body of Christ. The Head of the Church, the Lord Jesus Christ, is directing the activities of His Body in the world today, and He will receive all the praise and honor and glory for it.

Oh, there is a move of the Spirit of God, dear friends. But we can't just jump into it. *God* wants to get us there, and that is why we have to follow His *plans,* His *purposes,* and *pursue* them. In this visitation, Jesus told me, "This move will be lost unless the people are taught how to move *with* My Spirit."

There will be some who will read this and be just as lifeless as they ever were. Others will say, "Isn't that marvelous?" and do nothing to follow after God's *plans, purposes,* and *pursuits* for their lives. But there will be those people who will catch on and take hold of what the Lord is trying to get across to the Body of Christ in this hour, and *get God's plan for their lives* and follow after that! Those who do, will be ready for the move that God is wanting to bring upon the earth in this day.

The Body of Christ has not seen anything like what we will see when we get to that place where we have God's *plan* and *purpose*, not only for our own lives but also for the Church — and we are *pursuing* that plan!

Chapter 2
Plans, Purposes, Pursuits

As I've already mentioned, when this visitation with the Lord began, I kept praying out the words, "Plans, purposes, and pursuits."

When that last English word escaped my lips, I was caught away with Jesus. I began to see how men devise their own plans. Thoughts raced through my mind as I considered man's plans: Good — maybe thoroughly scriptural — but not God's plans for them.

In contrast to man's plans, I could see God's plan. The Lord spoke to me and said, "I bless all of My people as far as I can. But the reason there is not the move of God and the depth of the flow of the Spirit, and the fullness of the manifestation of the Holy Ghost today is because men do not take time to hear from Me. And they do not take time to follow My plan set forth in the scriptures. The more closely you follow My plan, the more My power will be in demonstration and in manifestation."

Many times, the reason people fail and the reason ministries fail is because they have the wrong plan, purpose, and motive.

Whatever you are doing for God, ask yourself, *Is this God's plan?*

A number of years ago, I was at a convention and afterwards several of the preachers were standing around talking. One minister, who was a pastor of a large church, said, "I'm thinking about resigning from my church, and going out in the suburbs and building a church." Then he said, "I'm going to build it around me." I watched the church he built, and I noticed that it never prospered. It *couldn't* prosper because it wasn't built according to God's plan. The pastor's *plans* and *purposes* were all wrong, so he *pursued* the wrong thing. A church ought to be built around *Jesus.*

When people's plans and purposes are wrong, it is even possible to split a church. Then some say that the Lord told them to do it! I don't believe God ever told anyone to steal another man's church members because I don't believe God is a thief. However, when a church does not follow God's plan, its members may leave voluntarily because they're not being fed spiritually.

That brings to mind a situation involving one of our RHEMA graduates, who went back to his home country of South Africa to start a church. He began with thirteen people attending a Bible study in his father's living room. They outgrew the house, so they rented a theater or as they are called in South Africa, a "cinema." In the process of time, they outgrew that. Finally, they rented a larger building and started RHEMA Bible Training Centre South Africa. Nearby, there was a Full Gospel church and the pastor was the national leader of a particular Full Gospel denomination. Although he had a congregation of 400 people, he had to work a full-time job besides pastoring his church.

This pastor kept cautioning his members not to go to the RHEMA graduate's church. He told them, "Don't go to that church because they're in error teaching that prosperity and faith business."

The man who related this to me said, "My family and I visited the RHEMA church, just to see what it was like. We liked it so well, we stayed!" In the process of time, 360 of this pastor's congregation also visited the church and liked it so well they stayed. Finally, this pastor had only forty people left in his congregation.

When we went to South Africa to dedicate the RHEMA graduate's new facilities, this pastor's Full Gospel denomination was holding a national convention at the time, and they sent us a telegram saying, "At first we thought what you were preaching was in error, but we've come to see that it is the truth. More power to you! We just want you to know that we're with you and we're for you."

The pastor of this denomination had finally seen that a church is supposed to support its pastor, and that he wasn't supposed to hold down a full-time job instead of devoting his time and energy to his own flock. He hadn't taught his congregation the scriptural principles about giving, but when he did, God prospered them.

Several years later, we returned to the RHEMA graduate's church, and the membership had grown so large they had to add on to the building! The RHEMA pastor had a congregation of about 11,000 members — approximately 2,500 of whom were black. How many white churches in America do you know that have 2,500 black members! Because of the success of this mixed congregation, one of the most prominent leaders in the nation called the RHEMA pastor in to his office, and said, "You seem to be the only one who has solved the racial problem in this country. Help us! Tell us how you've done it."

"Well," the RHEMA pastor said, "first you'll have to get everyone born again, because everyone — regardless of color — is selfish and self-seeking if they are not saved. But if you get people saved and get the love of God in them, you can change things in this nation!"

You see, this is God's plan and purpose for any nation — to get people saved, filled with the Spirit, and walking in the love of God. No matter *who* you are or *what* your endeavor is, if your plans and purposes are in line with God, they will succeed.

Because this RHEMA pastor's plans and purposes were in line with God, God has used him to be instrumental in networking more than 450 churches in South Africa! They are having a great revival and the Spirit of God is moving in a marvelous way.

I can remember another incident which took place many years ago when I was visiting another state. A pastor there had established a fairly large church and he hired an assistant to work with him. The church grew to a congregation of about 500, and the assistant pastor announced, "The Lord told me to start another church. I'm going to take 250 members from this congregation and start a church two blocks from here." Think about that! That's practically right on this pastor's doorstep!

That assistant pastor's *purposes* were all wrong! His church couldn't possibly prosper. Do you think God could bless that? No! God couldn't bless it because that assistant pastor was pursuing the wrong plan. Let's stay with God's plan. It will always prosper!

On another occasion, I was holding a three-week revival for a pastor who had all kinds of programs going on in his church. This pastor had put a great deal of pressure on me to find out what it would take to meet my budget, so I would come and hold this meeting for him. But in all my years of ministry, I never required anyone to give me anything. I never told a pastor he had to give me a certain amount of money in order for me to come and preach in his church. I would just tell the Lord, and He always supplied my needs.

Even though I didn't require it, this pastor guaranteed me a certain amount of money if I would hold this revival for him. After I arrived, he raised money in every service for every kind of project you could imagine, and he told me, "If we have any money left over, we'll give it to you." He had a little money left over, not nearly what he had said he would give me, and he gave that to me. I didn't say anything about it to anyone. I just looked to the Lord to meet my needs.

The pastor had me preach every Sunday morning of this three-week revival. After I got there, he also decided to hold extra services on Sunday afternoons. He said, "On Sunday afternoons, we can get people from all the other Full Gospel churches in the city to come to our meetings." His plans were all *man's plans* and ideas. Then he told me, "If we get people to come from all the other churches, we can raise a good offering." Not only were his plans and ideas his own, but his *purposes* were all wrong!

Never put money first! The first time the Lord appeared to me, He told me, "Be careful about money. Many upon whom I've placed My Spirit and called to the ministry have become money-minded, and have lost the anointing." We don't want to become money-minded and lose the anointing of God on our lives!

This pastor's *purpose* to have a Sunday afternoon meeting was to raise a big offering and get more *money*. As we were going into the third week of the revival, he announced to the people in that Sunday afternoon meeting, "We don't know whether we will go another week or not. Come tonight and we'll tell you." During the song service, he whispered to me, "I told the people that so we can get them to come back tonight. Then we'll tell them we're going on."

Just like someone was standing behind me — in fact, I looked around to see if there was anyone behind me — I heard a voice say, "When you get up to speak, tell the people you are closing the meeting tonight. And you close tonight."

I said, "Lord, I'm going to miss an extra offering if I do, and I'm going home and I will be off a little extra time. It takes so much money a week to meet my budget and I have no other income. Secondly, we haven't bought any Christmas presents yet, and I have a family to support. What am I going to do? I can't start another revival — not two weeks before Christmas."

The Lord said to me, "Don't bother about that; I'll take care of you." So I closed the meeting and I went home full of joy. The next week, the only time in all those years it ever happened, letters started coming in with offerings enclosed. (I think the most I had ever received in the mail at Christmastime was $36.) This week I received more than $300. It doesn't sound big now, but back then it was. One man wrote from California and said, "Brother Hagin, the Lord laid it on my heart to send you $150. That's not my tithe. I pay my tithes to my church where they belong. This is extra, and God told me to send it to you." Praise God — God saw me through!

I felt sorry for this pastor, though. He had ulcers and had requested that I pray for his healing. I asked the Lord, "Lord, what about him? What's going to happen to him?" Just as plainly as though someone were sitting behind me, the Lord said, "He has never asked Me for any kind of plan for his life, his ministry, or his church. He forms his own plans, and then he asks Me to bless them. I bless him as far as I can, but I can't meet his financial needs because he's putting forth his own plans and not Mine. I didn't tell him to do a lot of the things he's doing. He just added his own plans to what I did tell him to do. He tacks his plans on here and there, and I can't bless them. I would if I could, but I can't. I can't put My approval on man's plans when they are not My plans. And, you see, his purposes are all wrong. If his *purposes* are wrong, then his *pursuits* will be wrong."

Plans, purposes, and pursuits! It is easy to stray from God's plan. I believe many times that's the reason ministries get into dire financial trouble — they add to what God's plan was for them. They may be good things, even legitimate things, but they are additions to God's original instructions.

Remember, God knows the future better than we know the past. It pays in every way to wait before Him and get His plan. So many times we make our plans and then ask God's blessings on *our plans*. It's far better to get His plan, because His plan is already blessed. Get God's plan for your life and God's plan for your ministry. If you are a pastor, get God's plan for your church.

Stir Yourself Up To Find God's Plan

When God began to deal with me about the ministry He had for me, I didn't understand it.

I was pastoring a church, but on the inside something didn't feel quite right. I didn't know exactly what was wrong, but I knew something was wrong. I said to the

Lord, "Something's wrong; it feels sort of like washing your feet with your socks on." I began to do extra seeking of God and to stir myself up in prayer. *God* didn't stir me; *I* stirred up myself. I had always prayed quite a bit, but during this time I spent extra time seeking God with some fasting.

I said to the Lord, "Lord, something is wrong with me. I must be abnormal. I've got every reason in the world to be satisfied. This is the best church I've ever pastored. I've got the most money I've ever had, and we're living in the best parsonage we've ever lived in. My wife and I and our children are happy, and everything is just lovely. The Sunday school is running the most it has ever run in the history of the church. I ought to be satisfied. What's wrong with me?"

The Lord spoke up on the inside of me, and said, "What's wrong with you is that I never called you to pastor to begin with. That is not your calling."

Thank God, He allowed me to pastor for twelve years in His permissive will. And I learned some things through pastoring that I wouldn't have learned any other way. (I sometimes think evangelists, teachers, and ministers in the field ministry ought to be compelled to pastor at least two years. There would be a lot of things they wouldn't say or do. Then, too, I think pastors ought to go out on the field at least two years. They would discover some things about how to treat a guest speaker.) But I learned in that time of prayer that pastoring was not God's plan for my life.

When God told me He hadn't called me to pastor, I should have asked Him what He *had* called me to do! There is something about the Lord — there are just some things

He won't tell unless you ask Him because He is a perfect gentleman. No, He won't intrude upon you and interrupt you. The Holy Spirit won't do that either. When the Lord told me He hadn't called me to pastor, I didn't ask Him what He had called me to do; I just assumed that since I wasn't a pastor, I must be an evangelist. I just fell in line with the trend of the denomination I'd been associated with, and all they ever recognized were the offices of pastor and evangelist.

So I set out to be an evangelist. And I fell flat on my face. After one solid year of "evangelizing," I'd worn out my car and was afoot. We lived in a three-room apartment. Our son had to sleep on a rollaway bed in the kitchen in the winter and on the screened-in back porch in the summer. The children were inadequately clothed and inadequately fed.

Again, I sought the Lord. Something wasn't right. I still had that feeling that I was washing my feet with my socks on.

It's a long story, but the essence of it is, God was trying to get me to follow His plan for ministry. The Lord was trying to get me to teach.

EPHESIANS 4:11,12
11 And he gave some, apostles; and some, prophets; and some, evangelists; and some, pastors and teachers;
12 For the perfecting of the saints, for the work of the ministry, for the edifying of the body of Christ.

You see, I'm talking about *plans — God's plans*. We often do things because we think that's the way it ought to be done. But take the time to find out what God wants done!

Heaven has a plan for the Church in the earth. God was endeavoring to get me to move in line with His plan and His purposes not only for my life, but for the Body of Christ.

God had shown me the office of the teacher and I knew when that ministry gift was dropped upon me like a mantle from heaven. Yet when I prayed, I considered the circumstances of the religious thinking of the day. This was 1949 and 1950.

"Lord, they want me to preach. I can't get any meetings teaching. They want an evangelist. They want a revivalist. I can't make it teaching."

Yet I could not persuade Him. He had a plan. And only walking in the light of His plan could I know the fullness of His blessing.

During this prolonged time of seeking God, I started a meeting in Henderson, Texas, the last Sunday of 1949 which was held over into January 1950.

Finally, during this meeting, I said, "All right, Lord, I'll teach. I'll give you Friday night. That's our biggest crowd. I'll teach and I'll just prove to You it won't work."

We had been going one week and nobody had been born again; nobody had been filled with the Spirit. One little girl had lifted her hand for prayer.

So on Friday night, I *taught* forty-five minutes on the subject of faith. And I said to myself silently, *Now I'll give an altar call, even though I know nobody will come.*

Five grown men came to the altar and got saved.

I hadn't been able to sleep for praying, but after that I couldn't sleep for repenting!

By obeying *the Lord's plan,* in one service, four brand-new families were added to this church. In those days in

Pentecostal circles, if we had a three-week revival and got six people saved and two filled with the Holy Spirit, we thought we had a landslide! And here, by following the Lord's plan, this pastor got four new families in one night!

After this experience, I began to teach. God's plan for me was to teach and to stand in the office of the prophet as He wills. I went to another church and in ten days' time, twelve new families were added to that church. That happened again and again, because I had God's PLAN! I was carrying out God's purpose!

Plans! We do things sometimes just because we think that's the way they ought to be done. We think, *Well, this is the way our church does it. This is the way others do it, so that is the way we will do it.* No! Hear from heaven for yourself! There's no doubt in my mind that God has spoken to certain individuals to do some things a particular way. But they try to pattern their lives or their churches after what others are doing and they fail! Just because some pastor has a good program going in his church doesn't mean that same program will work in another church! It may not be what God wants at all; it may not be *God's plan* for that church.

You need to get down on your knees and find out for yourself what God's plans are for you, because God will only put His approval and His blessings on *HIS PLANS*. God's plan works so much better. If you get ahold of God's plan for your life or for your church, it will *work* and it will *produce results!* But if you try to build your house yourself, you will labor and labor. You may finally get it all built and it may *look* good, but it will all be in vain because the Lord wasn't in any of it.

If you pastors, for instance, will spend time seeking

God and waiting on Him, you will find that you will
become sensitive to the Holy Spirit. You will know what
God wants to do in your services. You will know exactly
what God wants to do. He is not going to bypass the leader
of the meeting! But if you're not that well acquainted with
the Holy Spirit so that you can know what He is doing,
then you are going to be left out.

I have said this many times — I think some preachers,
even Full Gospel, Pentecostal preachers wouldn't know
the Holy Spirit if they saw Him coming down the street
with a red hat on! He will start to move in their services,
and they just keep on with their little programs.

Being Out of God's Plan Brings Dissatisfaction

As I've already mentioned, I had pastored for twelve
years when I began to seek God about my ministry
because I was dissatisfied. Finally, Jesus said to me, "I
never did call you to pastor to begin with."

After a period of frustration trying to minister as an
evangelist, I again sought the Lord. He asked me, "What
are you going to do about what I said to you years ago
concerning fulfilling your ministry?"

I said, "Lord, I wasn't planning on doing anything
about that."

He said, "Well, you are going to have to or else."

I replied, "I believe I will!"

You see, something we need to realize is that being out
of the will of God brings dissatisfaction. Not only does
it bring dissatisfaction, but eventually, if we fail to correct
ourselves, we will have to reap the consequences of our
disobedience. No, God doesn't bring about those conse-

quences; they don't come from heaven. *"The THIEF cometh not but for to steal, and to kill, and to destroy"* (John 10:10). God simply has to allow it because we're not carrying out *His plan.* We're not pursuing *His purposes.*

Plans, purposes, pursuits! It's better to have God's *plan* and God's *purpose* and *pursue* that. Let's not follow our own plans! Let's stay with God's plan and purpose, and follow His pursuits! God's full blessing and the full dimension of the Holy Spirit can only come upon HIS PLAN! We must get God's best.

Chapter 3
Except the Lord Build the House

Except the Lord build the house, they labour in
vain that build it. . . .
— Psalm 127:1

Throughout more than fifty years of ministry, Psalm
127:1 has been the main scripture I've based my life upon.
Before I ever move to do anything, I make sure the Lord
is in it.

Notice in this scripture, that they *did* build the house.
They got it built, all right, but their labor was all in vain
because the Lord wasn't in it. So many times in the
ministry, what we do is good, but it is not the Lord's plan
at all. It is man's plan.

Psalm 127:1 refers to more than just building a house.
Of course, in the natural, if God is not in *whatever* you
are doing, it will fail. But the Bible is talking here about
spiritual things as well.

Whatever you are doing for God, ask yourself, *Is this
God's plan?* Remember, if the Lord is not building the
house, all your labor is in vain. You can build an entire
house and yet not have any part of it built according to
God's plan. This verse points out that *they* had to labor
to build it because *God* was not in it. Get God involved
in whatever you are doing. Find out what His plan is before
you ever begin to build.

It is easy to stray from God's plan. Ministers especially
are susceptible to straying from God's plan with
something which seems right, good, and legitimate. But
if God didn't tell them to do it, and it is not His plan for

23

them, they end up pursuing the wrong plan. When this happens, they forfeit the fullness of God's blessing.

For example, on October 1, 1979, we started Healing School on the RHEMA campus at the Lord's direction. Through the years, we've received marvelous testimonies from people who have been healed.

We had a custom of beginning these healing classes with someone leading singing. Many times, we would spend forty-five minutes just singing and worshipping the Lord. One day as I was going to Healing School, the Lord spoke to me. It was so real that it was just as if someone were walking beside me. The Lord said, "What is the purpose of this meeting?"

I answered, "It's a healing meeting."

"What kind of a healing meeting?"

"Well, we're teaching people who need to be healed how to receive healing and we are teaching others how to minister to the sick. That's the purpose."

"Then," the Lord said to me, "it's not a worship service."

"No," I said, "it's not a worship service."

"Then don't try to have a worship service. Only sing a few songs, just enough to get the congregation to participate, and go right into your teaching."

So we stopped conducting our Healing School as we had been. We got in line with God's plan. We sing and praise fifteen minutes or so, and then we go right into our lesson.

The area of worship was not the only place where we missed it in conducting our Healing School. Without realizing it, we drifted into the counseling business. Eventually, we built a building called the "Prayer and Healing Center," and we put in counseling rooms. People came by in person or telephoned for all kinds of counseling — marital, financial, spiritual, etc.

After a while, we could sense that something wasn't right. It seemed as though we were "washing our feet with our socks on."

So we prayed. My wife and I prayed with the leader of the Prayer and Healing Center. We asked the people who gathered regularly for prayer at RHEMA to pray with us about it.

One night during this prayer meeting, as I knelt beside a chair on the platform, the Lord spoke to me.

He said, "You've preached James 5:14 and 15 for years. Did you ever notice it is prayer and healing — not prayer, counseling, and healing?"

Of course you teach people the Word. That's what the lessons were about as we had the daily teaching on healing. But the Lord said to me, "Go look at the sign on the building. It says Prayer and Healing Center — not Prayer, Counseling, and Healing. I didn't tell you to counsel at all. You added that."

Then He said to me in just these words, "Don't counsel anybody except people of your own sheepfold. You can counsel employees and students at the school because that *is* your sheepfold. But do not counsel others. If they need counseling, they ought to be counseled in their own sheepfold. And if they do not have a sheepfold, that is where their problem is."

Thank God for teachers. Thank God for evangelists. Thank God for apostles and prophets. But we need the pastoral office. The shepherd *lives* with the sheep.

When I'm out in meetings, I encourage people: "Send

your tithes to your own church. The Bible teaches tithes *and* offerings. You can send me an offering if you want to, but keep your own church going."

You need the pastor. The crises of life come to all of us. The time may come when you or someone you know is in the hospital. You can call our office and we'll pray because the Bible teaches prayer. I won't come to the hospital, however. I can't, but your pastor will. (You may not have even been attending or supporting your local church. In fact, if it had depended upon you, the church may have been dead and bankrupt long ago.) But if you call your pastor, he'll be there to anoint you with oil and pray, and to stand with you in that hour.

Some of your kinfolks might die (God didn't say we'd live forever) and you might need people with you. Don't call me because I can't come. Or someone in your family may want to get married. Don't send for me or any other television or radio preacher because we can't come to marry them.

The local pastor attends to those matters. This is God's plan for the local church. But where the Prayer and Healing Center is concerned, God has a different plan, and we've got to follow God's plan for us. And in this case, we had to get in line with God by discontinuing outside counseling.

Another area in which I strayed from God's plan was in the format for our annual Campmeeting.

Many years ago, I began conducting meetings in Tulsa at the Sheridan Assembly Christian Center. The whole building wouldn't hold more than 800 people, and we usually had about 400 people who attended regularly. At night, local people would come and fill up the building. I used to hold crusades in that church — I'd just put on my own meeting and use their building.

One night I surprised myself (I surprise myself all the time saying things out of my spirit). I said, "This summer, we're going to have a faith seminar and an indoor camp-meeting. God said we are to start one." After I said it, I turned around and said, "Who said that?" and found that it had come out of my own mouth! I was speaking by inspiration; I never thought that up. It just came up out of my spirit.

Sometimes I'll say things by the Spirit of God, and my wife or Ken or Lynette will tell me what I said. I'll say, "I didn't say that — I know better." "Yes, you did!" they'll say, and when I go back and play the tape, sure enough, I said it!

The point is that the Lord gave us *His* plan and *His* purpose for Campmeeting, so we began to have a faith seminar and an indoor campmeeting. Then three years ago, the Lord spoke to me again about Campmeeting, because we had unconsciously drifted away from His *plan* and *purpose.*

I was praying about three o'clock one morning, and the Lord spoke to me, "When I told you to start having a faith seminar and an indoor campmeeting, I told you explicitly that the morning services were to be a faith seminar, the afternoon meetings were to be as the Holy Spirit leads, and the night services were to be the Campmeeting."

That was God's plan. But then, some way or another, without thinking, we had substituted our own plans, and had different teachers come in and teach on whatever subject they chose.

Young people don't understand about Campmeeting.

Some of the old-timers of Pentecost do. In fact, that's where we got the expression — from the old-timers. They'd come from all around and camp on the grounds. They'd come in wagons, and bring food along with them and hay for their horses. They'd just camp on the ground, and they were there all the time until the campmeeting was over. In our modern day, we're in such a hurry that we come in for a church service and stay for thirty minutes and want to go! But that's not campmeeting!

Campmeeting is a time when we all come together to enjoy the things of God and just relax in the Presence of God. We come away from our jobs and other distractions and just allow the Holy Spirit to do what He wants to do.

After the Lord spoke to me again about Campmeeting, we immediately began to implement His plan. We got back to His plan — not my plan or anyone else's plan.

A pastor once told me, "There's no telling how much money I've spent getting on planes and flying across the country trying to build my church. I'd hear of a pastor who was having success. I'd go there, learn how he did it, and then come back and implement that plan in my church. Instead of gaining ground though, I'd lose ground. The other fellow put that plan into effect and his congregation tripled. I put it into effect and lost twenty percent of the people. Since then, I flew across the country to another church and stayed one week, observed, and made notes. I went back to my church and adopted that plan. And I lost more people."

At the time I talked to this pastor, his congregation was one third of what it had been originally. "What am I going to do?" he asked me. He wanted me to give him a plan.

I said, "I don't know what God's plan is for you. Get alone with God and find out."

He said, "I don't have time — I'm too busy pastoring."

Dear friends, if you're too busy to wait on God to discover His plan, you may go through your entire life and everything you do will be in vain. Then what will you say to God when you stand before Him in eternity? He won't ask you about those things you did according to *your* ideas and plans. He will want to know what you did about *His plan* for your life.

The Secret of Success

A few years ago, I attended what was called an "Idea Exchange." Ministers from various churches and denominations across the country were invited to that meeting.

At that meeting, some of those ministers asked me, "Brother Hagin, what is the secret of your success?" One minister said, "When I first knew you, nobody had ever heard of you. You were preaching in small churches and, once in a while, in a large church. But then, all of a sudden, you became not only a national figure, but in just a matter of a few years — an international figure. Now how did that all come about? What is the secret of your success?"

I answered, "The only secret of success I know is walking in line with the Word of God, and praying and listening to the Holy Spirit. I simply listen to what the Spirit of God says to do, and then do it." Actually, everything I'm doing today is the result of believing the Word, praying in other tongues, and being obedient to what God told me to do.

Thank God for the value of praying in other tongues. Sometimes I interpreted my own prayers. In fact, that is how I first started interpreting — by interpreting my own prayers.

To tell you the real truth about the matter, praying in other tongues was instrumental even in showing me about my marriage and my children. I pastored a Pentecostal church in Tom Bean, Texas, in 1938 where I met my lovely wife. I was a 21-year-old pastor and I needed a helpmeet.

I was praying up in a barn loft that belonged to one of my deacons. I had been going with Oretha for a while at that point. I began praying in other tongues about my future, and I prayed this all out in other tongues. Then I prayed the interpretation out: I saw in the Spirit that I would marry her and that we'd have two children, and that's what happened!

I got that in prayer. I didn't get that because I was standing in the office of the prophet, because I wasn't at that time.

When you get down on your knees and find out for *yourself* what *His* plans are — because He will put His approval and His blessings on His plans — it works so much better. It will almost work like clockwork.

I remember how God dealt with me before the beginning of what has come to be called the Charismatic Movement.

In December 1962, I was preaching in a Full Gospel church in Houston. Suddenly, I felt a wind blowing upon me. It came with such force that it knocked me flat on the floor and I fell into a trance. (In Acts 10:9,10, the Bible says that Peter went up on the housetop to pray and fell into a trance.) All my physical senses were suspended.

I saw a beautiful flower garden surrounded with a white picket fence. In the middle of it was a pavilion or arbor. The garden was full of the most beautiful flowers of every kind. The arbor itself was made up of climbing flower plants. Each flower was in full bloom and was giving off a wonderful aroma. The perfume was visible as it rose into the air.

I came up from the east to the gate of the fence. Jesus was standing just inside. When I got there, He unlatched the gate, and pushed it open. He reached out His hand, took my right hand, led me inside, and shut the gate. Then He took my right hand in both of His hands, and led me down the path to the arbor.

Two white marble benches were on either side of the arbor. He sat on the bench to the south and without saying a word, pulled me down beside Him.

I looked around. From the west, I saw a river flowing into the garden. It was broad at its beginnings back up in the sky and it narrowed as it flowed into this little garden. As I looked, the river changed. It became people — people of every nationality, people of every dress and station of life. They were flowing into the garden.

I said, "Lord, who are these people? What does all this mean?"

Jesus said to me, "These are people from what you call 'denominational' churches and even from other religions of the world. In this day, I am visiting hungry hearts everywhere. I will visit places you never would have thought I would visit — not only what you call 'denominational' churches, but I will visit other religions where hearts are hungry and open to Me. These are people who will come into the light of the new birth and the fullness of being filled with the Holy Spirit. They will flow as one. The aroma that goes up is the praise of these people ascending into heaven, even as the incense of old ascended unto Me.

"You must play a part in this," Jesus said. "I want you to minister to the whole Body."

Jesus kept saying that: "I want you to minister to the whole Body," while I watched the following scene run off before me like you'd watch something on television.

I saw myself ministering in Baptist churches. I saw myself ministering in Presbyterian churches, in Methodist churches, in Disciples of Christ churches, and even in Roman Catholic churches — and I've done it! I saw people falling under the power and lying all around the front of Methodist, Baptist, Presbyterian, Catholic, and other denominational churches — and it has come to pass!

That might not seem so amazing to you now, but it was shocking to Full Gospel circles in those days. I was a Pentecostal preacher who preached strictly in Pentecostal churches.

That happened in December 1962. In January 1963, I was holding a meeting in another Full Gospel church in Houston. One night, a spirit of prayer suddenly fell on us. (We don't see that much anymore. In fact, we don't see it at all. You see, we only permit the Holy Spirit to go so far in Charismatic circles. But as we learn to follow God and really, truly worship Him, the Holy Spirit will be able to manifest Himself as He desires to.)

At this meeting in 1963, I was just preaching away and a spirit of prayer fell on us. Everyone hit the floor praying. *I* didn't tell the people to pray — the Holy Spirit just came upon the people to pray. I looked back across the congregation and no one was sitting on the pews. Everyone was either down around the altar praying or kneeling at their seats praying.

I stepped down off the platform, knelt by the steps, and began to pray. I had only been praying a short time when I was in the Spirit. For lack of a better word, I call it "getting lost in the Spirit," because time goes by and you think you've only been praying a few minutes but actually, you've been praying much longer.

By the time I finally opened my eyes and looked, I thought I'd been praying about fifteen minutes. I had not been conscious of anything else that went on around me, but actually I had been praying an hour and a half. I looked around and there was no one in the church except the pastor and me. I said to him, "Something happened to my watch. It must be running fast."

"No," he said, "that's the right time. I saw that you were lost in the Spirit so I didn't bother you."

Toward the end of my praying, I suddenly realized that I was doing something, so I opened my eyes. With my thumb and index finger, I had formed a circle. With the index finger of the other hand, I was tracing a circle inside those fingers. I'd go all around that circle one way, and then I'd come back around it, praying in tongues the whole time. I'd go three quarters of the way around the circle, and go back around, still praying in tongues. I'd go half way around it, then back again, still praying in tongues. I'd go a quarter of the way around, and trace it back again, praying in tongues. I thought, *What am I doing?* Then I began to interpret what I was praying about.

This was the interpretation: "You're going in a circle

in your ministry. You'll go all the way around that circle, and then you'll go back around it over and over again. (I was about to go back to a church where I'd been nine times before.) You'll go three quarters of the way around that circle, and then you'll go back three quarters of the way around that circle. You'll go half way around that circle, then you'll go back around that circle.

Finally, the Lord said to me, "Now get out of that circle. In fact, stop holding meetings in churches; go to a neutral place. Hold your meetings in a hotel or in a motel ballroom. Call your meetings 'All Faiths' Crusades' and invite people from any denomination to come."

Jesus explained why He wanted me to stop holding meetings in churches. He said, "One denomination is prejudiced against another denomination. Besides that, almost all Full Gospel churches are fishing out of their own bathtub anyway, and there aren't any fish in their bathtub." So I got out and went fishing for men, glory to God! We're enjoying the results of that today.

Then Jesus said, "Make another circle. That first circle represents your going to neutral places to hold meetings." Then I found myself making a little larger circle. Jesus said, "That second circle represents your putting into print all of your Bible lessons." We've done that. In fact, in English alone, we've published 37 million books. We are continuing to publish more than a million books every year. At the time, I didn't think it would be that big of a circle. Then Jesus said, "Third, put all of your messages on tape." At that time, we just had those old reel-to-reel tapes. Now we put out 40,000 cassette tapes a month.

Then Jesus said, "Get on radio and teach — don't preach." In those days, no one in Full Gospel circles was teaching on radio. They were all preaching. So I got on the radio and taught. Each time we'd break into one of those circles that I had prayed out, it would work so smoothly. Why? Because it was God's plan. We heard from heaven and the plan was blessed.

I've given just a brief overview of God's dealings in my life and ministry. But He doesn't just have plans and purposes for me. He has a plan for the Church. He has a plan and a place for each of His children, and His children can know His plans and pursue them in their lives and ministries.

But you have to get His plan from Him. You have to pray it through.

The old-time Pentecostals had a term, "praying through," but people misused it. They would say to a fellow believer, "Have you prayed through today?" Really, if you are in fellowship with God, you don't have to pray through, in that sense. However, if you are in a backslidden condition, you do need to pray through.

That expression got started because sometimes people do come up against forces of evil in prayer. You've got to pray through them sometimes. Daniel prayed twenty-one days until he prayed through. So sometimes there are *spiritual forces* that you have to pray through.

Sometimes you have to pray and wait on God to find out what *His* plans, purposes, and pursuits are. You need to find out God's plan for your life, your ministry, your church — or whatever it is that God has called you to do.

In waiting upon the Lord in prayer, all I did was simply obey what God told me to do. I haven't done anything except run to try to keep up with Him!

Once, a minister friend and his wife came to visit my

wife and me, and we were driving them around showing them RHEMA and all the facilities. They said, "You must be carrying a heavy load."

"No," I said, "I'm not carrying any heavy load. No, you're mistaken — I'm not the least bit burdened by anything. It wasn't *my* idea or *my* plan to start a training center. I didn't want to do it to begin with, anyway."

You see, I had already cast my cares upon the Lord. I had settled all this with the Lord and had His plan on the matter. Early in our building programs, I told the Lord about our financial needs. (The Lord is our friend and He is our Father. He cares about us, and He can understand us when we talk to Him.)

That's why I don't carry the burden! If it is the Lord's plan, He will put you over! *"Except the Lord build the house, they labour in vain that build it . . ."* (Ps. 127:1). And I know God can get the job done!

So what we are doing is the result of what *God* said to do, not what I wanted. It's not my plan or my purpose — it's God's.

Find Your Place of Anointing

One reason many ministers miss God's plan for their lives is that they try to be a "jack-of-all-trades and a master of none." We need to realize this — every one of us is limited! If you could do it all yourself, there wouldn't be any need for the rest of us. Yet some people seem to think, "If God takes *me* off the scene, the job won't get done!" Isn't it strange how God has gotten by without them all these years? No, it's human ego that likes to think that!

"Yeah, but I'm the only one who is doing anything for God!"

Dear me, many times it is the folks you have never heard of who are doing more for God than people with an attitude like that! You may not be gifted and anointed by the Holy Spirit to minister in a certain way, but find *your place* and you will be successful. If you don't know for sure where your place is, just keep giving people the Word and laying hands on them in faith! God honors faith, and you will have just as many miracles!

The late Rev. Howard Carter was the General Chairman of the Assemblies of God in Great Britain for nineteen years, and he built the first Pentecostal Bible school in the world. He was used by the Lord to minister some of the clearest teaching I have ever heard concerning the gifts of the Holy Spirit. I heard him say once that nearly everyone he laid hands on was filled with the Holy Spirit, and practically everyone his wife laid hands on got healed. You see, both he and his wife had found their place of anointing and they flowed together in their anointings as a husband-and-wife team in the ministry! They learned that by staying with their individual places of anointing, they were effective!

When people find their area of anointing and stay with it — not trying to be someone they're not — they become effective in whatever they are doing for God.

Sometimes God will show you what He wants you to do — you will have His plan. But at the same time, you will perceive in your spirit that the *time* to do it isn't quite right. Learn to wait for the right time to implement God's plan — wait for the quickening of the Holy Spirit. At other times, God will show you things in the Spirit, and although

you won't know *everything* God wants to do, as you fulfill
what the Lord told you to do — little by little, you will
move into deeper areas of the Spirit. As you are obedient
to follow God's plan and *His* purpose, He will begin to
illustrate and demonstrate some things to you and lead
you into greater understanding of His plan.

There will also be times when you simply pick up on
what the Spirit wants to do through others in the Body
of Christ, but that does not mean that God wants *you* to
do it.

Listen to what I'm saying. If you'll recall, sometimes
when Paul had something to say, he would say, "This is
what the Lord said." But at other times, he'd say, "God
gave me permission to say this."

Please get something clear in your mind: I'm speaking this by the Spirit of God because God wants to clear
up some areas so He can move in our midst. Many people
who have some sensitivity to the Holy Spirit sense what
God *is* doing and what He *wants* to do. They grab that
and run off with it and try to build something from that.
But because God didn't specifically tell *them* to do it, their
plans are only man's plan, not God's plan or purpose. They
add to God's plan or they take away from it, but they get
the real thing God wanted to do in a mess, and sometimes
they even thwart the plan and the move that God wanted.
We can't let that happen in what God wants to do in our
day in the Body of Christ.

How are we going to keep that from happening? Are
we going to pray? Certainly, we should pray, but that
won't do it. We are going to have to *teach* people what
the Bible says. We are going to have to get people
informed. The Body of Christ is going to have to begin

to follow after God's plans, purposes, and pursuits.

Let me use an illustration to explain what I mean. A number of years ago, I announced during Campmeeting that we were going to start a Bible school. Many other people sensed the same leading to start a Bible school. I'm sure God had probably spoken to some of these people; others were just sensing the move of God in that area and direction.

After we announced we were going to start a Bible school, we received many letters that said, "God told us to start a Bible school, but we don't know how. Could you tell us how?" Well, when God told us to start one, we didn't know how either. We had to seek *God's plan* for what *He* wanted *us* to do. We wrote these people back and said, "If God told you to start a Bible school, He'll tell you how to do it. If He doesn't tell you how to do it, He didn't direct you to start one in the first place!"

Then in another instance, I announced from the platform, "We are going to start Healing School." Right after that, we got letters from others who had also sensed the move of God in that area. They wrote us saying, "God told us to start a healing school. How do we do it? Tell us how to do it." However, when God told us to start ours, we had to seek Him for the "how-to." We prayed and sought God!

What happened was that many of these people sensed in the Spirit that God was moving this way, and they thought He wanted *them* to do it. They didn't take time to wait before God to get His plan for *themselves* or for their church.

When people sense which way God is moving, many times they assume God wants them to do something. Of course, there will always be those people who just want to start something because someone else is doing it. Most of them fall flat on their faces. Why? Because, *"Except the Lord build the house, they labour in vain that build it . . ."* (Ps. 127:1).

Once we get God's plan and begin to follow it, it is vital that we learn to rest in Him.

What happens so many times is that God really does tell Christians to do something, but then *they* try to go build it or do it *themselves*. They try to carry out God's plan in themselves and they do it in their *own* strength. They think *they* have to perform it, and some of them labor under that burden until the strain of it literally kills them; they have a heart attack and die young. Then you hear someone say, *"See,* that proves healing is not for everyone, because that fine fellow worked for the Lord, but he died right in the midst of doing God's will."

No, in that circumstance, if you do all the laboring to bring God's plan to pass, and you don't trust in Him to do it, you may work yourself to death! Seek God, and let Him bring His own plan to pass! When God tells you to do something, you need to rest as you go, glory to God! I'm resting *in Him!* The Bible says, *". . . we which have believed do enter into rest . . ."* (Heb. 4:3).

Chapter 4
What's Your Purpose?

"Even when men get My plan," Jesus said to me in that early morning visitation of 1987, "oftentimes their purposes are wrong.

"Some people get My plan," Jesus said. "I speak to them, but in trying to carry out that plan, their purposes become wrong. So I cannot bless them because man's purposes and pursuits must be lined up with My plans and purposes for the fullness of My blessing."

You can have the right plan with the wrong purpose.

Even in our individual church services and meetings, we can miss God's purpose and fall far short of His best. As I was caught up in the Spirit with Jesus, He told me that He has a plan and a purpose for every meeting.

"When it comes to having church, when it comes to services, when it comes to meetings," Jesus said, "men make their own plans and then ask Me to bless their plans. I bless them as far as I can, but I cannot put My full approval and blessing upon them because men are pursuing their own plans."

Then He spoke to me about the different kinds of meetings — believers' meetings, evangelistic meetings, healing meetings, teaching meetings, prayer meetings, worship services, and so forth.

He said, "Where you are missing it today in your culture in the United States is, you try to put all those kinds of meetings into one service, and so you never really reach the full potential of any meeting."

Sometimes in a campmeeting-type of setting, we have the time to combine many different kinds of services.

However, people in a church setting often try to have constant campmeeting, or all crusade-type services. You can't have campmeeting all the time. In order for people to get a balanced spiritual diet, they need all kinds of meetings. When we try to have all kinds of meetings in one, none of them are as successful as they should be. Then the Holy Spirit is hindered from moving like He wants to move because man is operating according to his own purpose and not according to God's purpose. Although His power will be in manifestation as much as possible under the circumstances, it won't be all that God has in store for us.

But if we'll learn God's purpose for each meeting and emphasize *that,* we'll have success in every meeting we hold. I'm reciting to you things that the Lord said to me during this visitation. I don't know about you, but some of the things He said to me corrected my thinking.

Believers' Meetings

One kind of meeting that we don't see much in the local church is a believers' meeting. People in the Early Church went to church because they *had* something. Today, most people go to church to *get* something. Well, if you have to go to church to get something, that's fine. But, really, Christians ought to bring something with them when they come to church.

We find believers' meetings specifically mentioned in scripture:

1 CORINTHIANS 14:26-29
26 How is it then, brethren? when ye come together, every one of you hath a psalm, hath a doctrine, hath a tongue,

hath a revelation, hath an interpretation. Let all things be
done unto edifying.
27 If any man speak in an unknown tongue, let it be by
two, or at the most by three, and that by course; and let
one interpret.
28 But if there be no interpreter, let him keep silence in
the church; and let him speak to himself, and to God.
29 Let the prophets speak two or three, and let the other
judge.

This is not talking about just any kind of service. It
is talking about a believers' meeting. Nobody is present but believers. ". . . *Brethren . . . when ye come
together . . .*" (v. 26).
First Corinthians 14:23-25, makes this plain:

1 CORINTHIANS 14:23-25
23 If therefore the whole church be come together into one
place, and all speak with tongues, and there come in those
that are unlearned, or unbelievers, will they not say that
ye are mad?
24 But if all prophesy, and there come in one that believeth
not, or one unlearned, he is convinced of all, he is judged
of all:
25 And thus are the secrets of his heart made manifest;
and so falling down on *his* face he will worship God, and
report that God is in you of a truth.

Here, in this passage, *believers* have come together.
The unbeliever might or might not come in. If he does,
the manifestation of God's Presence in the church is to
be so great that he will fall down before Him.
The closest thing I ever saw to this kind of meeting
was in 1939 and 1940 in a little church I pastored in
Farmersville, Texas.
This congregation was Pentecostal. As their young

pastor, I had recently come into Pentecost from the Baptists.

I would say that in 1939 and 1940, I probably didn't *preach* more than a half a dozen times on a Sunday morning; we had believers' meetings.

I came into Pentecost in 1939 and in those days, people thought you were backslidden if you didn't have a testimony meeting every service. We had a move of the Spirit in those days that the modern-day Charismatic knows nothing about. But we've got to get back to it.

In this church, primarily only our own people — believers — came on Sunday morning. Ordinarily, I'd just sit down on the platform and say to the congregation, "I'm going to turn this meeting over to the Holy Spirit. Whatever the Holy Spirit has given you, just get up and give it." Of course, if the meeting didn't run right, I was still responsible for it, and I'd get up and stop it or get it back into the right channel.

First Corinthians 14:26 says, "*. . . when ye come together, every one of you hath a psalm . . . doctrine . . . tongue . . . revelation . . . interpretation. Let all things be done unto edifying.*" How many believers are supposed to have something from the Holy Spirit? All of them! Of course, this will work better in a small church than it will in a large one. "*. . . EVERY ONE of you hath a psalm, hath a doctrine, hath a tongue, hath a revelation, hath an interpretation. Let all things be done unto edifying*" (v. 26).

I would tell my congregation, "Whatever the Holy Spirit has given you — give it. If the Holy Spirit has given you a song, just start a chorus. If the Holy Spirit has given you tongues for the whole body, speak it out. If the Holy Spirit gives you the interpretation, go ahead and interpret. If you have a prophecy, prophesy. Whatever the Holy

Spirit gives you — give it."

Remember, prophecy is *inspired utterance*. Because prophecy is speaking forth, there is an element of prophecy in testimonies. In these believers' meetings, people would get up and testify, and although they would sometimes start off speaking in the natural, they'd get inspired and their testimony would bless everyone. As they spoke, something would just go out over the whole crowd.

For instance, there was a man in the congregation who was very timid. Sometimes the Spirit of God would come upon him and with no music and no singing, he'd just get up and start dancing. You talk about dancing! It blessed everyone. And with no music! All we had was a piano in those days. Someone would start singing a chorus and the pianist would pick it up and start playing along.

We had three sections of seats in our little auditorium. There would be times when the whole congregation just sat quietly, reverencing and waiting on God. Sometimes the Spirit of God would move in such a way that with no pianist or any music at all, the people in one section would simultaneously jump up and start dancing all at once just like someone was leading them! There was no music and there was no one leading them, but they'd all start dancing just like some Unseen One was orchestrating them.

I'd sit on the platform, grinning and watching the Holy Spirit move. Then they'd all stop simultaneously and another section would get up and they'd start dancing with no one directing them. Then they'd all sit down again just like some Unseen One was directing them. The Holy Spirit was doing the directing! Then the people in the center section would all jump up and dance for a while and they'd all sit down at the same time. Sometimes, someone would get up and give a message in tongues. Most of the time, I'd interpret because I was on the platform and people could hear better that way. Once in a while, I'd encourage someone else to interpret the message.

God moved in some of the most unusual ways in those believers' meetings. But it was because we had real worship in our services — true worship. And we were careful to keep our worship in the Spirit and to reverence God and not get in the flesh. We didn't *put on* some kind of a demonstration, but there was a *demonstration of the Spirit* — there is a difference! We are not to *put on* a demonstration, but we are to allow the demonstration *of the Spirit.* Do you see the difference?

None of the services were alike. In some services, the Holy Ghost so came into the room and filled it with His Presence that nobody moved, nobody said a word. You were afraid to move or speak because a holy awe gripped the crowd.

We had no nursery. The babies were in their mothers' arms or asleep on the floor or on a bench. Little children were sitting by their mothers. Yet as we sat in total silence for an hour and a half, not a baby cried, not a child moved.

The Presence of God filled His temple. Ohhh! You carry that Presence with you for months and months.

Once in a while some unsaved person would come in. I remember one of those times. We were all sitting silently in God's Presence, when from the platform, I saw the back door of the auditorium open and a man come inside.

This fellow usually dropped his wife off at church on Sunday morning. Then he would go to an illegal gambling dive in town. He would come back around noon to pick up his wife because we were usually through by that time.

He told us later what transpired that day. He drove into the parking lot, rolled down the car window, and didn't hear anything. So he got out of the car and walked up to a window. We didn't have stained glass — we just painted the bottom pane of glass. He couldn't see inside, so he put his ear up against the window, but he couldn't hear anything.

He said, "I thought, *Perhaps the rapture has taken place and everyone is gone! The cars are all here.*"

He went back and sat in his car. An hour went by. It was one o'clock by that time and he hadn't heard anything.

We were all sitting in the Presence of God, almost afraid to move. We were engulfed in a holy awe, a holy atmosphere.

So he decided, *I'll just look inside to see if the rapture took place.* He'd been to church some and had heard preaching about the rapture, and his wife had also talked to him about it.

Sitting on the platform, I was the only person who saw him open the door and look around.

The building was about half full with most of the crowd sitting down toward the front. The back pews were empty, so he sat down on the very back pew as close as he could to the door.

Nobody said a word, not a child moved, not a baby cried — and we'd been there two hours! This move of the Spirit started just a little past 11:00 a.m. and when this occurred it was about 1:15 p.m.

Fifteen more minutes went by. I watched the man as he was looking around all that time. Suddenly, he started shaking violently. He got up and staggered down the aisle like a drunk man, shaking all the while, and fell across the altar calling on God.

No one went to the altar to help him pray. We all just sat there. We figured that what God had started in him, He was able to complete.

That didn't happen just once — it happened frequently. Almost every time an unsaved person would come in on Sunday morning, it would happen to them. They'd start shaking as though they had a chill. No one would say anything to them, but they would get up and come to the altar as the power of God came upon them.

We don't know too much today about the power of God in manifestation. Oh, we see the gifts of the Spirit operate sometimes, but God wants us to have all of it. He wants us to have His full plan.

The Lord talked to me about the manifestation of His power in the visitation in July. He talked about different kinds of meetings which Christians hold. He specifically mentioned believers' meetings.

If I were a pastor again, at certain times I'd have believers' meetings. These meetings would not be for the general public. Things can happen when just believers are present that should not happen in a meeting open to the general public. But if anyone else happened to come in, they would get saved just as they did in Farmersville, and they would encounter the Presence of God just as First Corinthians 14 says.

Evangelistic Meetings

We called our Sunday morning services in Farmersville, believers' meetings, because no one came except Christians.

On Sunday nights, though, visitors came and filled up the building. They even stood outside looking in the doors! We'd have more sinners than saints at those Sunday night meetings.

I would say to our congregation ahead of time, "We're coming tonight with the sinner in mind. We're not coming to worship God or to get blessed ourselves. We got blessed this morning. This isn't a believers' meeting. Some things which happened this morning would be out of order tonight. This is an evangelistic meeting. We're not interested in jumping and shouting, but we're interested in helping that unsaved one along."

We had good music on Sunday nights. Everyone appreciates good singing. There were solos, trios, and quartets.

People often told us, "You have the best singing in town." You see, they recognized the Holy Ghost anointing.

I preached an evangelistic message, and people were saved, filled with the Holy Ghost, and healed every Sunday night. It was just a common occurrence; we had constant revival.

People coming in from the outside, even sinners, would tell us, "When you step in the door here, you can sense the Presence of God."

You see, we had charged the atmosphere with the power of God that morning in the believers' meeting.

Prayer Meetings

We desperately need to get back to holding prayer meetings in our churches. Most of what people call prayer meetings today have deteriorated into little or no pray-

ing. What does "prayer meeting" mean? It means you
meet to pray. If you're going to call it a prayer meeting,
then that is the purpose of it. You should devote the major
portion of time to prayer.

I remember some time ago, a woman asked me if she
could talk to me after one of our seminars. She said,
"Maybe you can help me. I belong to a church and we have
a weekly prayer meeting. But I don't know why in the
world they call it a prayer meeting, because we very seldom
ever pray."

If people don't pray in a prayer meeting, they have their
plans and purposes all mixed up! She said, "Instead of
calling it a 'prayer' meeting, it should be called a
'prophesying' meeting because all they ever do is prophesy
over one another. Is that right?"

I said, "What do you mean, Is that right?"

"Well, for instance, they are always prophesying something bad to me."

I asked her, "What have they prophesied over you?"

"About eighteen months ago, they prophesied that my
mother was going to die within twelve months."

"Did she die?"

"No, she's in good health."

I said, "It's easy to judge that." Anyone with one eye
and half sense could tell that prophecy wasn't from God,
especially since her mother was still alive and well!

"Then they prophesied that my husband was going to
leave me within six months," she said.

"Did he leave you?"

"No, he didn't leave me. He doesn't understand
everything that's going on, but he is a wonderful man and
I love him and he loves me."

I said, "Well, that ought to be easily judged too."

If folks are having a prayer meeting, I don't know why they don't pray! I realize that it's good to sing a little at first to sort of get "tuned up." It helps to sing and worship God to get into an attitude of prayer. But in a *prayer* meeting, if all you're going to do is *sing* then you're going to miss out on God's plan and purpose for that meeting.

Not only do we need to hold meetings for the purpose of prayer, but everyone at the meeting needs to have a clear understanding of what to pray about.

I remember something I did in my ministry after I left my last church in 1949 and went out on the field. I was preaching primarily in Full Gospel churches, and it was the custom in those days in Full Gospel churches to close every meeting with the congregation coming around the altar to pray. I'll tell you, we need some more of those kind of services today! It would stop ninety-nine percent of all counseling in the church; people would get the answers to their problems while they are praying!

I'd purposely run polls on these people who came to the altar. I'd go along and tap them on the shoulder, and ask them, "What are you doing here at the altar?"

"Oh, just praying."

"What are you praying for?"

"I don't know."

If people don't know what they are praying for, how will they know if they get the answer? Yes, there is the kind of prayer where we are just waiting on God. But if that's what they were doing, they should have answered, "I'm not praying for anything specific; I'm just fellowshipping with my Father."

Since these people really didn't know what they were

doing at the altar, their purposes were wrong and they
didn't even know it. When man's purposes are wrong, the
blessings of God can only flow so far. God's blessings and
His stamp of approval can only be given in a limited way
when we are not in line with *His plan.* Get God's plan!
It's best!

So if it is important for *individuals* to know what they
are praying for, how much more important it is that we
have a purpose in mind when we meet *as a church* to pray!

I saw tremendous results in my own ministry as a
pastor when my church got in one accord and had the same
purpose in prayer. Let me share with you one such
instance.

The last church I pastored grew continually. That's the
way it should be with every church. We should be continually following God's plan, and reaching forth towards that.
This is the Biblical pattern for growth whether it is for
a church or for an individual.

The reason we were always growing in this church was
because we were continually trying to follow after God's
plan and to pursue that. For example, we were going to
hold a revival — so the *purpose* of the meeting was
evangelistic — to bring in the lost and get them saved.
In our church, we'd always had certain fast days and
prayer meetings set aside to prepare for special meetings
like this. Actually, we were just copying after what others
had done more than anything else. If we're not careful,
we can get in a habit of doing things that may be right,
but we're doing them just as a religious rite. If that's all
it is, it won't produce any results or amount to much.

Because I saw that we were just more or less following a religious form, I said to the congregation, "I don't

want you to even pray about the revival that's coming up."
I did that to get the people out of their religious rut.
   We were getting ready to hold an evangelistic meeting,
a revival — that was our main purpose. We were not going
to come to worship God, to have a believers' meeting, or
even to get blessed ourselves. We were coming for one
reason only, and that was to get the lost saved.
   I told the congregation, "When you come tomorrow
night for prayer meeting, write down on a piece of paper
the name of someone you want to see saved during this
revival meeting. If it is a husband and wife, write both
of their names down. If the person is a backslider or if both
a husband and a wife are backsliders, write down their
names. Write a 'B' on the paper so we will know they're
backsliders. You pray a little differently for a backslider
than you do for a person who has never been born again."
   Ordinarily, it doesn't happen in East Texas, but the
next night we had a cold spell and it snowed and sleeted.
People in Texas aren't used to that kind of weather, so
they don't go out in it. We didn't have as many people
come to prayer meeting as we normally did, but some
people did come. I collected all of the pieces of paper with
the names written down. I said, "First, let's pray according to the Word of God; after all, it's God's plan that
sinners be saved."
   We didn't have any music, singing, or worship because
that wasn't the purpose of this meeting; it was to pray. So I
said to the congregation, "Let's agree that these people will
have a revelation of Jesus as Savior during this revival
meeting. The Bible says, '... *if two of you shall agree on*
earth as touching any thing that they shall ask, it shall
be done for them of my Father which is in heaven'"

(Matt. 18:19).

We prayed for every name on that list; some of them we agreed on and some we prayed as the Spirit would direct us, and for some we prayed in tongues. After we prayed in agreement and claimed our answer, I said, "Now let's thank God for the answer. Once we thank God for the answer, don't pray about this again. If you think about it, just lift your hands and *praise* God for the answer."

Following God's plan, we got one hundred percent results! We knew exactly what kind of meeting we were having and we just pursued that! Everyone we prayed for except two were saved in that revival meeting! The other two were saved before the end of the year!

I left that church before the year was up and there was only one man we'd prayed for who had not been saved yet. However, before the year was over, I was preaching in California, and this man and his wife came up to talk to me after a meeting. They had moved out there, and he told me, "Brother Hagin, I want you to know that I'm your brother now. I've been born again!" That means before that year was over, we had one hundred percent success praying according to God's plan! I'd never heard of a prayer meeting that had those kinds of results. But, you see, we got in line with God's plan!

Unfortunately, not every pastor is willing to pay the price to have the right kind of prayer meetings in his church. I was holding a meeting for a pastor once, and he asked me, "Brother Hagin, how can I get my congregation to pray?"

I never did have any problem getting my people to pray. I said, "You pray yourself. You set the example for them."

"Oh," he said. He turned around and walked off. He was too busy doing other things to pray much. That's sort of like parents telling their children, "*You* shouldn't do that," when they do it right in front of their children themselves! Children will do just what the parents do, and act just like their own parents act.

Prayer is God's plan.

But men look for some human plan, some human formula, some "get-fixed-quick" scheme.

God hasn't got any "get-fixed-quick" plans. The new birth is instant, but spiritual growth is not. Spiritual development takes time.

We live in a time of fast food. All you need to do is to drive up to the window and get it. We live in a time of ninty-nine cent sales. But God is not putting on any ninty-nine cent sales. The things of God still cost the same price they did years ago. They never go up in price and never go down in value.

Pastors, get God's plan. Get down on your knees and stay there until you find out what His purpose is for your life and ministry.

Pastors are responsible to be the example for their flock to follow, and they are responsible for taking the time to prepare themselves so they can follow the move of God's Spirit. What often happens to some pastors is that when God does begin to move in their churches, they draw back from the supernatural instead of guiding it correctly and finding out what God's plan and purpose is for their church. Failing to follow God's plan and to move with Him kills the move of the Spirit. Then the church gets dry, dead, and dull, and splits in three or four different directions.

Some pastors are afraid to follow the move of God's

Spirit. They say, "I'm afraid of fanaticism and wildfire."
You know, if things get out of order, I've said for years,
"If there is wildfire in the church, don't bother about that;
there are enough wet blankets around to put it out." Most
of those folks complaining about wildfire haven't got any
fire at all! I agree with a statement I once heard another
minister say, "I'd rather have a little wildfire and God
moving, than have no fire at all and the order of a
graveyard."

If you're a pastor, what are you going to do if a prayer
group gets out of order? You need to do exactly what I
did. I took charge personally and began to direct them
rightly. We channeled that power in the right direction.
You talk about miracles! We had miracles every week in
our church. People were saved, filled with the Holy Spirit,
healed, and the miraculous was almost a common occurrence to us.

Even outsiders would call us for prayer. My wife and
I would pray for people who were not even members of
our church and who had never heard us preach one sermon! Yet, they'd come to us and say, "Sister So-and-so
told me how God uses you, so I thought if you would pray,
I would be healed." God healed them every time! The
reason God was using me like this, and the reason we had
the miraculous operating in our midst wasn't so much
because of me. It was that prayer group who was back-
ing me in prayer!

Really, I didn't know much back then. It's a wonder
some of the deacons didn't have to tell me to get in out
of the rain! But, you see, I was backed by a prayer group
that knew how to pray.

Pastors, don't back away from intercessory prayer

groups. Be there yourself and direct them. "Well, I don't
know how." That's where the problem is. Find out how
to lead people in prayer, but don't back off from this area.
If you are going to have the miraculous operating in your
church, you are going to have to have people praying. And
you are going to have to pray *yourself.*

Let's get God's plan on the matter! We see this kind
of prayer as God's plan in Acts chapter 4. You remember
the story: In Acts chapter 3, the man at the Gate called
Beautiful was healed. Peter and John were arrested for
questioning and were commanded not to preach or teach
in the Name of Jesus.

> ACTS 4:23,24
> 23 And being let go, they [Peter and John] went **TO
> THEIR OWN COMPANY**, and reported all that the chief
> priests and elders had said unto them.
> 24 And when they heard that, **THEY** [the whole company]
> lifted up their voice to God with one accord [they prayed],
> and said, Lord, thou art God. . . .

First, notice verse 23. When you get into trouble, it
is good to know what to do, isn't it? Go to people who know
how to pray. There's truth to the saying, "Birds of a
feather, flock together."

When Peter and John got into trouble, did they say,
"Man, we're in trouble! Dear Lord, we'd better get a com-
mittee together and go talk to the chief priests and elders
and see if we can't work this thing out"? No, they went
to those who knew how to pray! There is power in united
prayer!

Then in verse 24, it says, ". . . *they lifted up their voice
to God with one accord.* . . ." That doesn't mean every one

of them said the same thing to God in prayer. The Bible is saying that this is the Holy Spirit interpreting their prayer — this is the essence of what they were all praying in one accord. Everyone didn't say the same words by rote, but that is what they were all saying in effect in the Spirit, and that is the way God heard it.

The disciples didn't begin their prayer by talking about the problem. They didn't put the problem first — they put God first. They didn't start praying about the mess they were in and what a fix they were in because Peter and John had gotten arrested.

"We may all wind up in jail! Oh my, my, my, what are we going to do now? Momma told me I shouldn't get involved with that bunch. If only I'd listened to Momma!"

Is that what the disciples said? No, no, no, no!

They said, "... *Lord, THOU ART GOD* ..." (v. 24). Aren't you glad He's God? No matter what happens, He is still God! No matter how dark it looks or what kind of mess it looks like you're in, God is still God!

ACTS 4:23-31
23 And being let go, they went to their own company, and reported all that the chief priests and elders had said unto them.
24 And when they heard that, they lifted up their voice to God with one accord, and said, Lord, thou art God, which hast made heaven, and earth, and the sea, and all that in them is:
25 Who by the mouth of thy servant David hast said, Why did the heathen rage, and the people imagine vain things?
26 The kings of the earth stood up, and the rulers were gathered together against the Lord, and against his Christ.
27 For of a truth against thy holy child Jesus, whom thou hast anointed, both Herod, and Pontius Pilate, with the

Gentiles, and the people of Israel, were gathered together.
28 For to do whatsoever thy hand and thy counsel determined before to be done.
29 And now, Lord, behold their threatenings: and grant unto thy servants, that WITH ALL BOLDNESS they may speak THY WORD.

(That kind of praying brings results! They didn't pray, "Lord, grant that we'll be able to make an agreeable compromise with them." No! No!)

30 By stretching forth thine hand to heal; and that signs and wonders may be done by the name of thy holy child Jesus.
31 And when they had prayed, the place was shaken where they were assembled together; and they were all filled with the Holy Ghost, and they spake the word of God with boldness.

Some people get excited when the power of God comes on people, and they shake or fall under the power. You wait until the building starts shaking — then they will really get excited!

In Acts 5, we find the answer to their prayer.

ACTS 5:12-16
12 And by the hands of the apostles [remember they prayed for signs and wonders] were many signs and wonders wrought among the people; (and they were all with one accord in Solomon's porch.
13 And of the rest durst no man join himself to them: but the people magnified them.
14 And believers were the more added to the Lord, multitudes both of men and women.)
15 Insomuch that they brought forth the sick into the streets, and laid them on beds and couches, that at the least

the shadow of Peter passing by might overshadow some
of them.
16 There came also a multitude out of the cities round
about unto Jerusalem, bringing sick folks, and them which
were vexed with unclean spirits: and they were HEALED
every one.

Isn't that strange? Sick folks who were vexed with
unclean spirits. "I thought all spirits had to be cast out?"
No, they were healed every one. Glory to God, everyone
that Peter's shadow fell on, was healed. God is God! And
He always will be! He's still GOD! He still works the same
way now that He did here with the Early Church.

Why is it so important that we have the proper kind
of prayer meetings in our churches? Because there's a
move of God on! God is wanting to restore the supernatural operations of His Spirit in our local churches.
Actually, He began to start a wave of intercessory prayer
a few years ago, but some people became misguided and
thwarted it.

Hear me carefully, now. Back in the beginning of the
'80s, we changed some things as far as the government
was concerned through intercession and we got some right
people into office. But then the Body of Christ let up on
that prayer, and some people went to the extreme and got
into the ditch on intercession. It hindered the true move
of God and it made people draw back from entering into
the intercession that God wanted for the Body of Christ.
In fact, some churches split over the issue of intercession.

One pastor in California told me his church split three
ways, because some of his intercessors got the "revelation" that God was through with him at that church and
that he was supposed to leave. *He* hadn't heard God tell

him to leave. A third of the church stayed with him, but it split the church wide open.

You can readily see why this pastor was not very interested in any kind of intercessory prayer, because the intercessors are the ones who messed him up. They divided the church. Actually, no group of intercessors should be praying by themselves, unless they have some mature person over them who understands the move of God's Spirit. Otherwise, they will get off every time. They fail to realize that when the Holy Spirit is moving the most — that is exactly when Satan gets in.

I'm saying this to you because the Lord has said to me that unless Christians turn situations around in our nation, and get the right people in office in the next election — in just a matter of two to three years — our living standard will be half of what it is right now because of the economic conditions.

We can change that by prayer! There is a work to be done in the earth and there is a harvest to be reaped. There is a wave of revival and glory that is coming not just here in the United States, but across the world! And the devil is not going to stop it!

So let's get in tune with the *purpose* of God and restore prayer meetings in our churches to what He intends for them to be. We'll see powerful results when we do!

Teaching Meetings

God also wants us to have teaching meetings in our churches where the primary purpose is just to teach the people. In such services, we need to keep singing at a minimum. Remember, it is not a worship service, although there should also be times when we meet just to worship God. But in a teaching meeting, we should endeavor to turn the service right over to the speaker, because the purpose of the meeting is primarily to *teach* — to impart truth from God's Word. When we pursue *God's purpose* in spiritual matters — then we know what to do in each service.

Pastors and all ministers should ask themselves this question: What is the purpose of this meeting? What is God's plan?

You see, it's not a matter of just "having church." We've got to have God's *plan* and *pursue* it with His *purpose* in mind. This means we may have to spend time waiting upon Him to get His plan and purpose.

Once we understand what He wants us to do, we must flow with Him in the outworking of each service.

His Purpose or Ours?

I remember one particular Mother's Day when I was pastoring the church in Farmersville, Texas. I had worked hard on a Mother's Day sermon that year. I mean I worked on it *for days.* I had quotes of great and famous men of old — I quoted Benjamin Franklin and Abraham Lincoln and men like that. I had all my notes and I worked hard on them. When I was finally finished, I knew that sermon was a good one!

There were four other churches a few miles away that were putting together a special afternoon meeting on Mother's Day. They wanted me to come and preach. Because of that, I missed my morning service, so I told my congregation we'd have our Mother's Day service on

Sunday night instead of on Sunday morning.

When I preached that sermon in the afternoon for these other churches, I knew it was good because everyone just bragged on it! So I thought, *I'm going to preach that Sunday night in my church.*

I planned my evening service so that everything was about "Mother." There were special songs all about *Mother.* There was a ladies trio singing about *Mother.* However, the whole time that the ladies trio was singing, I didn't hear one word they sang because the Lord was dealing with me. There was an argument going on between my heart and my head.

The Lord said to me, "Have a healing service right now. Just as soon as they finish that song, get up and announce a healing service."

"Why, Lord," I said, "You're going to ruin my good sermon. Lord, I worked on this thing for days and weeks. I can't preach a Mother's Day sermon next Sunday — it won't be Mother's Day. The people would think I was crazy! I'll have to wait a whole year before I can preach my sermon." *My sermon!*

The Lord said again to me, "Pray for the sick just as soon as the singers finish singing."

I said again, "Lord, the people will think I'm crazy." I looked over the crowd. In the Mother's Day program, we were going to have some of the younger children come to the platform to do some recitations, and their fathers had come to see their children perform. I knew some of those men wouldn't be back in church again until the Christmas program!

So I said to the Lord, "Lord, those men will think I'm crazy. I mean, we have everything planned to focus on

'Mother.' I've got this Mother's Day sermon, and it's a good one too. It's all about 'Mother' in the Bible. This crowd will think I'm crazy getting up here announcing a healing meeting and praying for the sick. Nothing is going in that direction, Lord! Everything is directed toward 'Mother.' "

The Lord said again, "Pray for the sick. Minister to the sick."

After that ladies trio finished their song, I got up and opened my Bible. I even began reading my text on "Mother." Finally, I just closed my Bible and said, "I'm going to obey God. God said, 'Minister to the sick.' "

I remember in that service there was one fellow who would frequently come by our parsonage. Actually, he would cut through the yard between our parsonage and the church to go to a store up the street.

I don't know what had happened to him, but somehow he had injured his back in such a way that he walked stooped over. He couldn't straighten up and walk normally. When I announced the healing service, he came forward for prayer. I laid hands on him and the power of God hit him and instantly straightened his back and he stood up straight! He was an older man, but after God healed him he could twist around, bend over, and even touch the floor. He went through all kinds of gymnastics right in front of everyone. In that service, a little baby was also miraculously healed. I looked back in the congregation to the men I thought would think I was crazy for having a healing meeting, and they were all crying. They were wiping tears from their eyes!

You see, when we pursue God's *purpose* rather than our own, the Holy Spirit is free to move in our midst. He

can accomplish more in five minutes than we could
accomplish in five years!

Right Purpose, Right Motive

Another important aspect of pursuing God's purpose
has to do with our attitudes and motives. Did you know
you can have the right purpose with the wrong motive and
never succeed? Let me illustrate what I mean.

In 1947 there came a healing revival here in America
which lasted through 1958. Several years before it came,
God stirred me up to pray. I didn't know anybody else
was praying; however, I am sure they were for this is God's
way. God's plans are prayed through first.

I was seeking God because the only manifestation of
the Spirit we had in our services was tongues and interpretation.

I said, "Lord, here in First Corinthians chapter 12, are
all these other manifestations of the Spirit. But about all
we ever see manifested are tongues and interpretation."

Thank God for tongues and interpretation, but let's not
stop there. That is not all of it.

I said, "Your Word reveals three power gifts: special
faith, working of miracles, and gifts of healings. These
should be in manifestation among us."

(First Corinthians chapter 12 teaches nine manifestations of the Spirit [vv. 7-11]. These can be divided into three
groups of three: the *revelation* gifts — word of wisdom,
word of knowledge, and discerning of spirits; the *power*
gifts — special faith, gifts of healings, and the working
of miracles; and the *utterance* gifts — prophecy, tongues,
and the interpretation of tongues.)

I prayed almost every night about this matter. Sometimes at three or four o'clock in the morning, I'd get up and pray an hour or so. In the winter, I'd go into the living room to pray by the heater. It was too cold to kneel on the bare floor in the bedroom because there was no heat in that room.

On three occasions, I woke up kneeling by the couch in the living room, and I didn't remember going in there. I said to myself, *How did I get here? I must have come in here in my sleep.*

I prayed about nothing other than the manifestation of the power gifts among us. I did not pray that God would use me, because I really preferred that God would use anyone else except me.

Many prayers for the supernatural workings of God are not answered because men's purposes are wrong. Oftentimes men have in mind, *God use me.*

I did not pray that He would use me. I couldn't have cared less whether He used me or not. I wanted people to be blessed and helped, for the Church to be enhanced, and for the glory to be given to God.

At that time, I prayed that these things would come into manifestation as they are revealed in God's Word. I knew they belonged to us. I prayed that we would have a prolific manifestation of these power gifts, and I just persisted in my praying.

One day, I went to my little study in the church to prepare the Sunday sermon. But I was so burdened to pray that I got out of my chair and started praying. I prayed approximately five hours in other tongues.

It was the longest I'd ever prayed in tongues at one time. I'd get up only to go next door to the parsonage for a drink of water, or to move around a little because I was on my knees all the time. But I counted only the time when I was actually in prayer.

I said, "Lord, I've been praying about the manifestation of Your Spirit, but I don't know what to pray for as I ought. So I'm praying in tongues, in the Holy Spirit, depending upon You to help me pray this thing through."

God wanted to manifest Himself, and I knew how to pray in a measure. But I still didn't know how to pray as I should. Today, we don't know exactly how to pray either. There's a move of God upon us. God is wanting to manifest Himself through signs and wonders to the world. We know to pray, and yet we don't know how to pray as we ought (Rom. 8:26). So we must rely on the Holy Ghost.

After approximately five hours into my prayer, I hit a "gusher." Glory to God! The Holy Ghost gave me a word of wisdom.

Some people say, "I don't ever get anything."

I know. You never stay long enough in the Presence of God to get anything. By the time it comes, you're gone.

When this word of wisdom came, I grabbed my pad and pencil and wrote it down: February 1943. I still have the original note. Here is what it said: *At the close of World War II, there will come a revival of divine healing to America.*

God's plan was revealed four years before it came!

The next year, I preached that at a young people's rally in Longview, Texas. I gave the date and told them what God said would happen. When I made this public announcement of God's plan, the power of God fell on the crowd. Every preacher ran to the altar. Every person present — both young and old — hit their knees praying. The glory fell on us.

It happened just as God had said: In 1947 the healing revival started.

Eventually, there were 120 ministers in what we called "The Voice of Healing." Every healing evangelist in America of any stature except Brother Oral Roberts was in it. *The Voice of Healing* magazine edited by Gordon Lindsay reported the revival, and we used this magazine as a medium of advertisement.

Now here is the point I want to get to, and Jesus talked to me about it in the recent visitation. I had to lay a foundation, however, for you to see it. You see, you can get God's plan, but your purpose can be wrong in carrying out His plan.

There was an outstanding healing evangelist in "The Voice of Healing." He was a man called of God and anointed by the Spirit. He had God's plan for the hour and God's plan for his life. He was equipped with supernatural equipment to fulfill the ministry God had given him. As the Spirit willed, the Holy Ghost manifested Himself through this man in some of the most miraculous things I've ever seen.

I saw blind eyes instantly opened through his ministry. I saw a person — the only one I've ever seen with this disease — whose body had begun to petrify. This dear one was carried into a meeting lying like stone on a stretcher, but was instantly delivered and arose and walked. It was a marvelous sight to behold.

Once my wife and I were traveling and we stopped by to visit one of his meetings. A state home for the deaf was nearby, and they had brought in five men who could neither hear nor speak. Each one, right down the line —

one, two, three, four, five — was instantly healed before
everyone's eyes.

The minister immediately got up and started receiv-
ing an offering and the anointing left.

His purpose was wrong. You can't use God's plan to
raise money.

The Lord said to me about that same minister, "You
go tell him he is not going to live much longer unless he
judges himself." The Lord told me to tell him he must
judge himself in three areas. One of those areas was about
money. I did not go to this minister, and God dealt with
me about that. But this minister never judged himself and
within three years, he was dead at a young age.

Your purpose has to be God's purpose.

I trust you get the message of Jesus' appearance to
me. A mighty move of God's Spirit is coming and we must
keep our purposes right. We must pursue God's plan —
not man's — with God's purpose.

You cannot use the things of God to raise money. You
can only tell people what God has told you and give them
an opportunity to be in on it so that fruit may abound to
their account (Phil. 4:17). I tell people, "God said to start
RHEMA Bible Training Center." But I put no emphasis
on money. I tell people what we're doing and give them
an opportunity to help if they want to and if they can. You
have to be very careful in this area.

Jesus once said to me, "Many upon whom I have placed
my Spirit and have called to the ministry have become
money-minded and have lost the anointing."

Ohhh! I don't want to lose the anointing — not for a
second, not for a minute. Every minister, every preacher,
every singer, and every person called of God must be

careful along these lines. We cannot take God's plan and pursue a different purpose. We have to pursue *both* His plan and His purpose.

Not only do we need to be careful about our motives concerning money, but we must beware of human ego.

Years ago at a Voice of Healing Convention, I heard a pastor say something that caught my attention. He was a good pastor and had established a good work. But it was in the days of revival — especially tent revivals. Healing evangelists were everywhere, and tents were everywhere.

This pastor said, "If Roberts [speaking of Oral Roberts] can do it, I can do it."

Was that God's plan and purpose for him? Or was it his human ego speaking? As a young man just in my thirties, I made a mental note of it and watched him to see what would happen.

He left his church and got a tent. And he did it. For a little while he did it almost as well as Brother Roberts. He had a 5,000-seat tent and finally got up to a 10,000-seat tent. But then he went down, down, down.

During this same time, I was also in "The Voice of Healing," but God said to me, "You stay in the churches." And I stayed in them from 1949 until 1962, until God gave me a different plan.

I traveled from church to church, preaching constantly. I was in meetings ninety-five percent of the time. And in practically every meeting — I don't mean it happened occasionally; I don't mean it happened once in a great while; I mean in almost every meeting — someone would stand up and prophesy that I was to get a tent.

"I've got a word for you. God wants you to get a tent."

God no more wanted me to get a tent than He wanted

me to fly to Mars. And I didn't get one.

Why did they do that? They did it because everyone else was getting a tent. I watched many other ministers get a tent because people prophesied that they should. The tent, the minister, and the ministry folded up.

You don't do something because someone else is doing it. Find out what God wants *you* to do.

Why am I saying all these things? Why did the Lord Jesus visit me when He did and speak to me about *plans, purposes,* and *pursuits?* It's because He wants to move again in this day with supernatural manifestations! The move of God does not just belong to the revivals of the past! You see, there was a great revival and outpouring of the Holy Spirit that started in 1906 in the old Azusa Street Mission in Los Angeles. By 1907 that wave of revival began to spread nationally and internationally. Then in 1947, forty years later, the wave of the Healing Revival started. You talk about healing! I got in on it, and to tell you the truth about it, it was the easiest thing in the world to get people healed. I have never seen anything like what we had then; it was easy to get people healed!

A lady evangelist (really, she was more of an exhorter) once told me the same thing. She said, "My husband and I were in the ministry. He would play the piano and we would both sing, but I was the main preacher. We had been in the ministry for more than thirty years, but we had never laid hands on anyone in all that time. We would just hold meetings, get people saved and filled with the Holy Spirit, and exhort them a little. But when this wave of healing came along and everyone was laying hands on folks for healing, we decided we would try it too.

"The first person I laid hands on," she said, "was

totally blind and was instantly healed! Dear Lord, it almost scared me to death! It was the easiest thing in the world to get folks healed. It was just like healing was 'in the air.' We had some of the most miraculous things happen you ever saw in your life!''

A healing wave like this is coming to the Body of Christ again. There will be miraculous healings like this in this next move of God! We need to know the wave is coming, and we need to know how to prepare ourselves to be effective in it. That is the reason I have recorded in this book what Jesus said to me in the visitation of 1987. He said that the Body of Christ is to get *His* plan, *His* purposes, and *pursue* that!

Chapter 5
Walking in the Light

The reason many churches never prosper and many ministers never fulfill the call of God upon their lives is because they don't follow God's plan — not only His plan spoken to their hearts by His Spirit, but also His written plan, the Bible. When the light of God's Word comes, it shows us God's plan for each one of us.

A good example of what can happen when a person walks in the light of God's Word can be seen in the ministry of Fred Price, Pastor of Crenshaw Christian Center in Los Angeles, California. Fred was faithful to walk in the light of God's Word as it was revealed to him.

I remember the first time I ever met Fred. Back in the early '70s, we were conducting a seminar in Albuquerque, New Mexico. My attention kept being drawn toward a nice-looking black man sitting in the congregation. I finally asked my son-in-law, "Who is he?"

My son-in-law had met Fred Price and he explained that Fred was a pastor who had come across some of my books. He was so hungry for God that he had read every one of them. When he learned that I was going to be in Albuquerque, he came to the meeting to check us out.

During the course of that seminar, Fred approached me and asked, "Would you come to a black church even if it's small?" I said, "I'll go anywhere God says to go." I'm not tied to anything. If God says go, I'm going to follow *His* plan.

So I held a meeting in Fred's church, and to tell the truth about it, I hadn't been in a building that small for a long time! His main auditorium seated 150 people, and he had a little side room where a few folks could be seated. So many people came to the meeting that they had to stand behind the platform! In the course of time, his church grew to about 300 people and he had to buy a bigger building. The new building seated 1,200.

Over the years, Fred kept following God's plan and walking in the light of it and today, he has more than 15,000 members. That's quite a little growth!

"Yes, but that's just because God sort of took a liking to him."

No, it's because when the light came, he walked in it! You see, the entrance of God's Word gives light! The light of God's Word reveals God's plan for the individual believer and God's plan for the Church!

The reason some folks seem to be just *partially* blessed — blessed only in a limited measure — is because they're just *partially* walking in the light of what God has for them. Others refuse entirely to walk in the light. For example, I heard one preacher say about a particular Biblical principle, "Bible or no Bible, I'm not in favor of it." I'm in favor of *everything* the Bible says! I don't want to fall short in any area of the Bible!

Can you understand why God has blessed some people only so far? Have you ever noticed that with some moves of God, when the waves of blessing come, some people only seem to go so far and even then, there are those who "die on the vine," so to speak? It's because they don't *walk on* in God's plan. Or sometimes the plan that they are walking in is all right for the day, but it is not the *full revelation* of the Word of God *or* of God's plan for them. Then, too, once that wave reaches its crest, if people are not careful, they will ride that thing in to the shore and become dry and dead. No, get on the next wave that is coming, hallelujah! If you don't, the time will come when God will have to almost withdraw His Presence, because you won't *walk on* in the light.

It's not enough simply to have God's plan in a directional sense. You must also walk in the light of His Word which has already been revealed to you, practicing it in all areas of your life and ministry, and you must continue to walk in any further illumination which He gives you. The plan of God won't be fulfilled in your life — even though you may have clear direction concerning the future — if you refuse to obey His written Word.

Likewise, the plan of God will not be unveiled to you in a further measure unless you are willing to move on with Him and to undergo change. You see, some people get comfortable where they are. They become comfortable in a particular location or position. They become comfortable with the knowledge they have of God. It takes effort and often sacrifice to continue to pursue God and His plan. That's another reason why some people reach a point of stagnation and never progress in their lives and ministries past a certain point — they're not willing to pay the price to go further with God.

Let's never reach the point where we become complacent about practicing the Word of God in our lives. Let's never get so comfortable where we are that we're unwilling to change in order to move forward with God. God will always be moving forward. I want to go with Him and be in on everything He wants to do in this hour!

Let's walk in the light and fully accomplish the plans and purposes of God!

Chapter 6
A Change in the Order of Worship

As I stated previously, God is always moving forward. His plan is a progressive plan. As we study the Bible, we see God's plan being gradually unveiled, beginning in the Old Testament and increasing in clarity and fullness until the end of the New Testament. This is a truth that the majority of Bible scholars accept.

For example, we see types and shadows of a promised Redeemer throughout the Old Testament. However, it is not until the gospels of the New Testament that Jesus of Nazareth is unveiled as the fulfillment of those Old Testament types and shadows. And the fullest understanding of His death and resurrection is not realized until we get over into the Epistles.

I said all that to say this: In the visitation of July 1987, Jesus showed me something about the progression of worship from the Old Testament to the New Testament. He directed me to John chapter 4:

> JOHN 4:23,24
> 23 But the hour cometh, and now is, when the true wor-
> shippers shall worship the Father in spirit and in truth: for
> the Father seeketh such to worship him.
> 24 God is a Spirit: and they that worship him must wor-
> ship him in spirit and in truth.

John chapter 4 relates that Jesus was passing through Samaria when he stopped at Jacob's well in Sychar. When one of the women of the city came to the well to draw water, Jesus asked her for a drink.

> JOHN 4:9
> 9 Then saith the woman of Samaria unto him, How is it

that thou, being a Jew, askest drink of me, which am a
woman of Samaria? for the Jews have no dealings with the
Samaritans.

Samaritans were half-breed Jews. Aside from the racial
differences between Jews and Samaritans, there were differences regarding the worship of God. Both groups worshipped God, but they worshipped in different places.

In the course of Jesus' conversation with the woman
at Sychar, she asked Him about a key issue which
separated the Samaritans from the Jews in religious worship: "... *Sir, I perceive that thou art a prophet. Our
fathers worshipped in this mountain; and ye say, that in
Jerusalem is the place where men ought to worship"* (John
4:19,20).

When the woman said, *"Our fathers worshipped in this
mountain ...,"* she was referring to Mount Gerazim, a
mountain significant in the worship of God throughout
the first five books of the Old Testament. The Samaritans
believed that Mount Gerazim was the proper place to worship, and this was where the Samaritans were worshipping during the time of Jesus' earthly ministry.

However, the Jews had designated Jerusalem as the
place to worship God. This designation was made after
the temple was built there and the Shekinah Glory of God
appeared in the temple. It was a requirement that every
Jewish male, thirty years and older, had to present himself
before God at the temple in Jerusalem at least once a year.
Therefore, during Jesus' earthly ministry the Jews went
to Jerusalem to worship God.

The woman at the well, perceiving that Jesus could
speak with authority, wanted Him to tell her where the

proper place of worship should be. Jesus' answer revealed to her that neither the Samaritans nor the Jews were right because the order of worship was changing.

> JOHN 4:21-24
> 21 Jesus saith unto her, Woman, believe me, the hour cometh, when ye shall neither in this mountain, nor yet at Jerusalem, worship the Father.
> 22 Ye worship ye know not what: we know what we worship: for salvation is of the Jews.
> 23 But the hour cometh, and now is, when the true worshippers shall worship the Father in spirit and in truth: for the Father seeketh such to worship him.
> 24 God is a Spirit: and they that worship him must worship him in spirit and in truth.

Jesus said to me in the visitation, "Really, in so many words, she asked me, 'Who is right? The Samaritans or the Jews?' And in so many words, I answered her, 'Neither is right. Because the time is coming and now is, that they that worship God must worship Him *in Spirit* and in truth.' "

The time had not been right to worship in Spirit and in truth before the ministry of Jesus. In fact, the Old Testament saints *couldn't* worship God in Spirit because they didn't know the Spirit of God as we do. Only the king, the priest, the prophet, or someone especially called by God to perform a certain task, had the Presence of God *upon* them or *with* them. The prophet, priest, and king had an anointing from God that came *upon* them to stand in those offices. Anytime God called someone else to do a certain work, an anointing of the Spirit came *upon* them to perform that task. None of those we might term "the laity" had the Spirit of God *upon* them or *in* them. And not one of the anointings in the Old Testament was the same thing that occurs under the New Testament when people are born again and have the Spirit of God dwelling *on the inside* of them.

In the Old Testament, those who believed in God did not have God's Presence abiding *within* them. That is why they had to present themselves in Jerusalem where God's Presence was. The temple in Jerusalem was God's house where His Presence dwelled. But in the New Testament, *we* are God's house: believers are the temple of God. God's Spirit lives in us individually, and He lives in the Body of Christ collectively!

Jesus pointed the Samaritan woman to a new time — to a new age in the order of worship. It would be an age where saints would be able to worship God *in Spirit* and in truth because the Spirit of God would be living on the inside of them! Jesus Himself was ushering in that new order of worship.

By His reply, Jesus indicated to the woman that because of what God was wanting to do in that hour, He was not putting His approval on the way either Jews or Samaritans worshipped God. Spiritually speaking, the time had come for a change in the way God's people worshipped Him. It was time for the way man worshipped God to change from Old Covenant to New Covenant. Jesus was ushering in a New Covenant and a new way of worship. The time had come for man to be indwelled by the Holy Spirit so he could worship God in the Spirit.

Even in natural life, there comes a time when things change. In your own life, weren't there times when things changed for you? For example, when you got married, didn't things change in your life? When your first child was born, things changed, didn't they? There comes a time for change, both in the natural realm and in the spiritual realm. Certainly a change as dramatic as the change between the Old Covenant and the New Covenant would affect the way man related to and worshipped God.

Jesus said to the woman, ". . . *the TRUE WORSHIP-PERS shall worship the Father in spirit and in truth: for the Father seeketh such to worship him"* (John 4:23). What God is seeking in the dispensation of the New Testament is *true* worshippers.

We can't go back to the Old Testament and worship God like they did and be *true* worshippers. We can't go back to the Old Testament and carry on our services like they did and be *true* worshippers. No, Jesus said, ". . . *the hour cometh, and now is, when the true worshippers shall worship the Father in spirit and in truth . . ."* (v. 23).

Yes, people in the Old Testament worshipped God in all the fullness they could under the Old Covenant, but we have a New Covenant — we *can* worship God in Spirit and in truth!

You find expressions in the Old Testament where people worshipped *before* the Lord and worshipped with all *their* might. That's because their worship was in the flesh only — they didn't have the Spirit. They couldn't worship *in* the Spirit or *in* the Lord; they could only worship *before* the Lord. They couldn't worship in the power and might *of the Holy Spirit;* they could only worship with all *their* might. In order to be a true worshipper of God *who is a Spirit,* we must worship *in the Spirit!*

Under the New Covenant, everything we do in worship must be in the Spirit. We should not try to go back under the Old Covenant and worship like they did. People under the Old Covenant were spiritually dead — they had not been born again. The salvation of the Old Testament saints was not complete until Jesus' death, burial, and resurrection. We who are born again should worship as those who are alive unto God! We should worship in the power of His Spirit!

"You won't worship God like your forefathers did in this mountain," is what Jesus was saying to the woman at the well. "And neither will you worship Him like the Jews have worshipped Him heretofore in Jerusalem. Now, the true worshippers shall worship the Father in Spirit and in truth."

The order of worship has changed from the Old Covenant to the New Covenant. In order to be true worshippers living under the New Covenant, we must follow the New Covenant order of worshipping *in the Spirit.*

Chapter 7
Dancing in the Flesh
or in the Spirit?

When I was caught up in the Spirit with Jesus on that July morning, I found myself standing with Him above the ceiling of the Tulsa Convention Center. As we looked down upon the crowd, I saw that many people were dancing. Jesus said to me, "It is unscriptural in the New Testament to dance before the Lord. It *is* scriptural to dance in the Spirit."

Dancing before the Lord is done in the flesh. God is a Spirit. We cannot worship Him, a Spirit-Being, using fleshly means. Jesus said in John chapter 4 that the Father was seeking true worshippers who would worship Him in the Spirit.

What many people are doing by dancing without the anointing of the Spirit is something that Jesus spoke to me about at length: they are substituting brass for gold. What do I mean when I say they are substituting brass for gold?

In the Old Testament, Solomon built the temple or the house of the Lord, and he made all the utensils out of gold. Later, the gold utensils were taken out of the temple, and King Rehoboam brought brass into the Lord's house in their place. He substituted *brass* for *pure gold.* Notice that in the construction of the Lord's house, the Scriptures say it was fashioned with "pure gold." It was not only gold; it was *pure* gold. But brass isn't a pure metal; it's an alloy consisting of copper and zinc, and Rehoboam substituted *that* for the *pure gold* that had been in the temple.

1 KINGS 6:20-23,28,30

20 And the oracle in the forepart was twenty cubits in length, and twenty cubits in breadth, and twenty cubits in the height thereof: and he overlaid it with pure GOLD; and so covered the altar which was of cedar.

21 So Solomon overlaid the house within with PURE GOLD: and he made a partition by the chains of GOLD before the oracle; and he overlaid it with GOLD.

22 And the whole house he overlaid with GOLD, until he had finished all the house: also the whole altar [this is referring to the house of the Lord] that was by the oracle he overlaid with GOLD. . . .

23 And within the oracle he made two cherubims of olive tree, each ten cubits high. . . .

28 And he overlaid the cherubims with GOLD. . . .

30 And the floor of the house he overlaid with GOLD, within and without.

1 KINGS 7:48-50

48 And Solomon made all the vessels that pertained unto the house of the Lord: the altar of GOLD, and the table of GOLD, whereupon the shewbread was,

49 And the candlesticks of pure GOLD, five on the right side, and five on the left, before the oracle, with the flowers, and the lamps, and the tongs of GOLD,

50 And the bowls, and the snuffers, and the basons, and the spoons, and the censers of PURE GOLD; and the hinges of GOLD, both for the doors of the inner house, the most holy place, and for the doors of the house, to wit, of the temple.

2 CHRONICLES 12:9,10

9 So Shishak king of Egypt came up against Jerusalem, and took away the TREASURES of the house of the Lord. . . .

In these verses, we see what the treasures of the house

of the Lord were — everything was made of gold.

> 9 ... and the treasures of the king's house [This was
> Solomon's own house]; he took all: he carried away also the
> shields of gold which Solomon had made.
> 10 Instead of which king Rehoboam made shields of
> BRASS, and committed them to the hands of the chief of
> the guard, that kept the entrance of the king's house.

As Jesus and I were standing above the crowd talking, He said to me, "In this Charismatic move, Christians
have brought the brass of the world into the temple of the
Lord as a substitute for pure gold. What they have is a
mixture; it's not pure. Therefore, I can only bless My
people so far, because they've substituted brass for gold.
They've brought the clapping and the dancing of the world
into the temple."

[Of course, we realize that in the New Testament the
temple of the Lord is the Church — the Body of Christ,
not a building made with hands.]

Jesus continued, "You see, when you come into the
New Testament, you find that all praise and worship is
to be done *in the Spirit.*" The Old Testament saints worshipped God purely in the flesh. We in the New Testament
are to worship God *in the Spirit.*

We are living under a New Covenant established on
better promises. Therefore, we should not go back to the
Old Covenant and copy what they did, nor should we copy
their form of worship.

There's something we need to understand: Though the
principles and *examples* in the Old Testament may
be the same as in the New Testament, the *practices* are
not the same.

Someone may say, "Well, David danced before the Lord." Yes, he did, but that was in the Old Testament. In the New Testament, we don't dance *before* the Lord — we are to dance *in the Spirit.*

Let me explain it this way: In the Old Testament, we do find scriptures about dancing. For example, Psalm 149:3 says, *"Let them praise his name in the dance. . . ."* You can also find reference to dancing in Psalm 150:4: *"Praise him with the timbrel and dance. . . ."* And the Bible says, ". . . *David danced before the Lord* [Does it say that David danced in the Spirit? No!] *with ALL HIS MIGHT . . ."* (2 Sam. 6:14). David danced before the Lord with all of *HIS* might.

Jesus said to me, *"David danced before the Lord with all of HIS MIGHT."* Whose might? *David's* might! Dancing before the Lord was part of the pattern for Old Testament worship.

As I've already mentioned, the Bible is progressive revelation. David, living under the Old Covenant, danced before the ark of the covenant as it was returned from Philistine captivity. That ark, at that time, was the only place on earth where God's Presence dwelled.

God's Presence had dwelled in the ark since Moses had built the tabernacle at God's command:

> EXODUS 25:1,2,8,17,21,22
>
> 1 And the Lord spake unto Moses, saying,
> 2 Speak unto the children of Israel, that they bring me an offering. . . .
>
> 8 And let them make me a sanctuary; that I may dwell among them. . . .
>
> 17 And thou shalt make a mercy seat of pure gold. . . .

21 And thou shalt put the mercy seat above upon the ark;
and in the ark thou shalt put the testimony that I shall
give thee.
22 And there I will meet with thee, and I will commune
with thee from above the mercy seat. . . .

Moses pursued the plan of God exactly as the pattern
was given to him. And the day came when the work was
completed.

EXODUS 40:33-35
33 . . . So Moses finished the work.
34 Then a cloud covered the tent of the congregation, and
the glory of the Lord filled the tabernacle.
35 And Moses was not able to enter into the tent of the
congregation, because the cloud abode thereon, and the
glory of the Lord filled the tabernacle.

The Presence of God, the Shekinah Glory, was manifested in the earth according to God's plan and according
to God's purpose.

However, because of the sin of the Israelites, later in
Israel's history, their enemies — the Philistines — were
able to capture the ark of God.

David, a man after God's own heart, became king and
with God's help, he defeated the Philistines. Then he arose
and took people with him to bring back the ark of God
(2 Sam. 6:1,2).

But the first time David attempted to bring back the
ark, he made a mistake. He had the right plan and even
pursued it with the right purpose. But he did not pursue
it God's way. In transporting the ark, he substituted man's
plan for God's revealed plan. He set the ark of God upon
a new cart (2 Sam. 6:3).

The Companion Bible has an interesting note on this detailing why David's attempt to move the ark of God on a new cart proved unsuccessful:

Note #3: A New Cart. This was contrary to the Divinely prescribed law (Num. 4:15; 7:9; 10:21. Deut. 10:8. Josh. 3:14. 2 Sam. 15:24. 1 Chron. 13:7; 15:2, etc.) When the Philistines did it in ignorance (1 Sam. 6:7) no judgment fell on them because the Law of Moses was not delivered to them. But David should have known: hence judgment came. The solemn lesson is that anything introduced into the worship of God contrary to His requirements is deserving of His judgments. This includes all that is contrary to John 4:24, and all that is of the flesh, which "profiteth nothing" (John 6:63). All this is like David's "new cart" and is sin in God's sight.*

Also, God's Word had instructed the Israelites that the *"service of the sanctuary"* belonged to the sons of Kohath. They were to bear the ark upon their shoulders. (*See* Num. 4:15; 7:9.)

On their first journey, the oxen stumbled and shook the ark. When Uzzah put forth his hand and took hold of it, the Lord broke forth upon him.

2 SAMUEL 6:6,7

6   And when they came to Nachon's threshingfloor, Uzzah put forth his hand to the ark of God, and took hold of it; for the oxen shook it.

7   And the anger of the Lord was kindled against Uzzah; and God smote him there for his error; and there he died by the ark of God.

The next attempt to transport the ark was successful.

David handled the ark of God's Presence according to *God's plan* and David received God's blessing. Living under the Old Covenant, he did indeed dance with all *his might* before the ark of the Presence of the Lord.

Later, David's son, Solomon, built "... *the house of the Lord at Jerusalem in mount Moriah ...*" (2 Chron. 3:1), where the Presence of the Lord was shut up in the Holy of Holies. As I already mentioned, much pure gold was used in what was then the house of the Lord in the earth. Like Moses before him, Solomon finished the work.

> **2 CHRONICLES 5:1,7,13,14**
> **1   Thus all the work that Solomon made for the house of the Lord was finished. ...**
>
> **7   And the priests brought in the ark of the covenant of the Lord unto his place. ...**
>
> **13   It came even to pass, as the trumpeters and singers were as one, to make one sound to be heard in praising and thanking the Lord; and when they lifted up their voice with the trumpets and cymbals and instruments of musick, and praised the Lord, saying, For he is good; for his mercy endureth for ever: that then the house was filled with a cloud, even the house of the Lord;**
> **14   So that the priests could not stand to minister by reason of the cloud: for the glory of the Lord had filled the house of God.**

And again as happened with Moses' tabernacle — the first dwelling place of God in the earth — the glory of the Lord also filled Solomon's temple.

The Lord instituted for Israel what He called, "My feasts" (Lev. 23:1,2). There were certain requirements for the men of Israel in keeping these feasts: *"Three times in the year all thy males shall appear before the Lord God"* (Exod. 23:17).

In order for them to appear "before the Lord God," they had to go where the ark of God was. These three feasts are referred to in the original Hebrew of Exodus 23:17 as *regalim. Regal* is the Hebrew word for foot, and *regalim* is the plural, feet. In other words, you were to take your physical feet and walk to where God's Presence was.

That is why they had to go to Jerusalem to worship God (after the building of Solomon's temple). Because then the Holy Presence of God was kept shut up in the Holy of Holies in Solomon's temple in Jerusalem. Nobody dared approach that Holy of Holies except the high priest, and he did so only under great precautions. Otherwise, he'd fall dead.

But when Jesus died on the cross, the New Testament tells us, "... *the veil of the temple was rent in twain from the top to the bottom* ... " (Matt. 27:51). God no longer would dwell in temples made with hands.

After the death, burial, resurrection, and ascension of our Lord Jesus Christ, the Epistles written to the Church reveal that *we,* the Church, are now the house of God.

> **1 CORINTHIANS 3:16**
> 16 Know ye not that ye are the temple of God, and that the Spirit of God dwelleth in you?

> **2 CORINTHIANS 6:16**
> 16 And what agreement hath the temple of God with idols? for ye are the temple of the living God; as God hath said, I will dwell in them, and walk in them; and I will be their God, and they shall be my people.

> **HEBREWS 3:6**
> 6 But Christ as a son over his own house; whose house are we. . . .

1 TIMOTHY 3:15
15 But if I tarry long, that thou mayest know how thou
oughtest to behave thyself in the house of God, which is
the church of the living God, the pillar and ground of the
truth.

Now, through His Spirit, God lives in men — not in
man-made buildings.

David, living under the Old Covenant, danced with all
his might *before* the Presence of the Lord.

Today, living temples of the Living God dance *in the
spirit.*

We need to get the difference clear in our minds
between Old Testament worship done in the flesh, and New
Testament worship done in the Spirit. There is a difference
between dancing in the Spirit and putting on a show in
the flesh or dancing to keep time to the music. When you
are truly dancing in the Spirit, you don't even need to have
music. Many people in church services are just dancing
to the music. Maybe you've jumped around a little like
some people do to keep time with the music. But that's
not dancing in the Spirit — that's substituting brass for
gold. You don't have to have music to dance in the Spirit.

Neither do you need to have people present to watch
you dance because your dancing is not a production for
man's eyes, but an expression of your heart toward God.

I've heard about some churches that are holding
dancing classes to teach people to dance in order to worship God! You can't teach people to dance to worship God
any more than you can teach people to speak with tongues
to worship God!

Someone may say, "Well, you can teach people to
sing!" Yes, but there is scripture in the New Testament

which speaks of singing in worship to God. Even though people may practice to sing in church, they don't sing the devil's songs in a worship service.

Also, did you ever notice this? When someone is singing, whether they're singing with a choir or singing a solo, you can close your eyes, get your mind off the person, and focus your attention on worshipping God. You can't close your eyes and worship God when someone is performing a dance — all your attention is focused on them.

Teaching people to dance in the Spirit is no more than cheap brass! Can you imagine having a class to teach people to speak with tongues! You can't teach people how to speak with tongues. You can teach them how to be born again and you can teach them how to yield to the Holy Spirit, but the Holy Spirit is the only One who can give them utterance.

People are trying to worship God in church with interpretive dance and ballet. Friends, you can't interpret the power and move of God with a dance. There's no scripture for that. That's substituting brass for gold.

The things of the Spirit can only be interpreted by the Spirit. And the Holy Spirit has plainly set forth the ways He demonstrates Himself in First Corinthians chapter 12. The full import and blessing of God *cannot* and *will not* rest upon us as long as we substitute brass for gold in the temple of the Lord.

Many dancers and even their ministers will say they're worshipping God. But if they were sensitive to the Holy Spirit, they could tell that He gets grieved with such fleshly display. I've been a guest in services where the Presence of God actually lifted when people began to perform those theatrical dances.

Besides, have you ever noticed that it's only the skinny women who do the ballet and interpretive dancing? If that kind of dancing was of the Spirit, anyone could dance that way — skinny and fat people alike — and it would bless everyone. I've been in services where fat people danced in the Spirit and the whole congregation was blessed.

You see, when people are truly dancing in the Spirit — no matter who they may be — something like a sweet-smelling incense goes out over the crowd. But when this worldly type of dancing goes on, the congregation gets to watching those dancing and their attention is not on the Lord.

I'll tell you another thing. Christian men have commented that the costumes worn by female dancers and their body movements while performing "interpretive" dances were so sensuous that the men had to look away. That is even true of many women who dance to the music in church services. I can't believe that dancing which causes that kind of response in men is of the Spirit of God. I'm just being honest with you.

Pastors are going to have to teach their people to bring pure gold back into the temple and to get the brass out! Brass looks like gold; you have to examine it closely to tell the difference. But God wants pure gold, and we should too.

We do not go back under the Old Covenant and pick up their dances to worship God under the New Covenant, and we do not bring the brass of the world's dances into the Church.

It is important to note that there is not one word in the New Testament about dancing *before* the Lord as a form of praise and worship. However, the New Testament does emphasize being filled with the Holy Spirit, so that our worship and praise is carried out *in the Spirit*. And if you know the move of the Spirit of God, you know that the Holy Spirit moves on you sometimes to dance *in the Spirit* — and sometimes He does get in your feet! But the Holy Spirit is not motivating people who are just putting on a show *in the flesh*.

When dancing is done in the Spirit, it blesses everyone. When it's done in the flesh, it blesses no one. Oh, it may look good and people may say, "Isn't that beautiful?" But it's a substitute for the real thing. There's a real anointing to dance, and it's by the Spirit *as He wills* — not as we will. It is true that we must will to yield to Him, but the unction to dance comes from Him: it's a dance *in the Spirit*.

I dance in the Spirit very often, but I don't just put on something. Unless the anointing is there, I don't do it. That would be like trying to give a message in tongues with no anointing. We've all seen that. It's just dead, and it deadens the service.

In many of our meetings when God is moving to heal and bless people, there are just some folks who can't discern anything. They speak out or do something without the anointing. If we don't teach them, they will get themselves and the service in a mess.

I can illustrate the difference that dancing in the Spirit will have upon a service as opposed to dancing in the flesh by sharing some true stories with you.

Years ago when I was pastoring the church in Farmersville, Texas, we saw a woman from another church virtually raised up from a deathbed in one of our Thursday night services. Doctors had said she would be dead in a matter of a few days, but God healed her. The following Sunday, she attended our church.

I had this sister testify in the Sunday morning service and tell about her miraculous healing. That Sunday night during our evangelistic service, she was back again and there were outsiders and sinners present. I wanted them to hear her testimony, so I said, "Sister, stand up and give us your testimony."

She was sitting over to one side in the congregation, so she stood up and told how her husband had admitted her to three different clinics, but every doctor said the same thing: "We can't do a thing for you. You'll be dead in a matter of a few days." Then she told how God raised her up on Thursday. When she said that, she started dancing. You talk about dancing in the Spirit! I got up and went to the pulpit and preached my sermon. She danced all the way through my sermon. I gave the altar call, and she danced all through the altar call. We didn't have any rugs on the floor — we didn't even have enough money to buy rugs in those days — we just had wooden floors. But that little lady never made a sound as she danced! Sinners who had come to that meeting talked about it for months.

The next Saturday, she told us that she'd had to buy a new pair of shoes, and she showed us the pair of shoes she'd worn when she danced in the church. These shoes had just been bought the day before. She'd danced the 1/4-inch leather heel right off, yet no one ever heard a sound, and she never interrupted the service! I kept right on preaching. I couldn't even tell that she was dancing unless I looked over at her. That's a miracle in itself!

More recently, in one of our crusades, some people in

the congregation got up and started what looked like a square dance right in the middle of a special song by the RHEMA singers! It quenched the move of the Holy Spirit immediately. God's Spirit was grieved. He had been moving in a marvelous way in the service, but when those people started square dancing, the congregation quit worshipping God or even listening to the singing. It just threw a damper on the whole service.

The Holy Spirit moved on one of our singers and he began to exhort the crowd that square dancing is *not* in the Spirit. Then the Holy Spirit came on him and he started dancing in the Spirit, and it brought the anointing back. Again, you see, the people brought brass into the temple of the Lord instead of gold. They substituted brass for gold!

When you look at the two — brass and gold — you can hardly tell the difference, can you? You've got to examine them closely to be able to tell the difference. But God wants *pure* gold!

During the visitation before Campmeeting when Jesus and I were standing above the crowd, I looked down and saw what would be the Wednesday night service of Campmeeting. I saw Buddy, my son-in-law, dancing in the Spirit, and I saw myself dancing in the Spirit. I also saw someone out of the crowd dancing in the Spirit. I didn't know who it was, except that it was someone who had never danced in the Spirit before but had always wanted to.

The next week at Campmeeting all this came to pass! Buddy danced in the Spirit just like I saw him doing! I simply acted out what I had already seen myself do. Then because I had seen it come to pass in the Spirit, I said to the people, "There's someone who has never danced in the

Spirit, but you've always wanted to," and I pointed to the section where I'd seen someone dancing in that visitation.

A young man stood up and I said to him, "When I point my finger at you, the Holy Spirit will come upon you. Just go ahead and yield to Him. When the Holy Spirit comes upon you — you'll dance in the Spirit." I pointed my finger at him, the Holy Spirit came upon him, and he took off dancing in the Spirit!

There is a difference between dancing in the flesh just because *you decide to* and dancing in the Spirit *under His unction*. I'm just telling you what the Lord said to me; you can do with it what you want. What you do with it is up to you. Don't come fussing to me about it; all I know is what Jesus, the Head of the Church, said to me: "It is unscriptural to dance before the Lord in the New Testament. But it is scriptural to dance in the Spirit."

I'm speaking by the Spirit of God when I say that bringing brass into the temple grieves Him. Jesus said to me as we watched some people in the Campmeeting services dancing in the flesh, "I'll bless them because they are My children and I love them. But I can only bless them so far — they cannot have the full measure of My blessing."

I don't know about you, but I'm not satisfied with settling for second best from God! I want the best God has in every service. I want the FULL MEASURE of His blessing. I want the full flow of God's Holy Spirit to be in manifestation, don't you?

The Companion Bible (Grand Rapids: Zondervan Bible Publishers, reprinted by permission of The Bullinger Publications Trust, 1964, 1970, 1970), p.415.

Chapter 8
Reverence: Key to God's Presence and Power

When I first looked at the luminous dial of the clock in the early morning hours of Thursday, July 16, 1987, it read three o'clock. When I looked at the clock after the visitation, it was seven minutes before six o'clock.

In the intervening hours, I'd been caught away in the Spirit. In Revelation 1:10, it says that John was "... *in the Spirit on the Lord's day* ..." and that he saw Jesus.

We know very little about being in the Spirit to tell the real truth about the matter. We get anointed with the Spirit to pray or to preach. But that is not what John meant when he said he was in the Spirit on the Lord's day. When you're in the Spirit — and I've been there several times — you don't really know right at the moment that you're even in the natural. Because you are in the Spirit — in the spirit realm!

I was in the Spirit on the morning of July 16, and I saw Jesus. I saw Him just as plainly as I could see you if you stood before me. I was caught up with Him to a place above the Tulsa Convention Center, and we were looking down upon what I knew was our upcoming Campmeeting which would begin Monday, July 20.

Although we were above the building, I could see into the auditorium.

I saw one of the services unfold before us. Jesus narrated as I looked on. I saw all of us in the auditorium as we were taking part in the service. As I looked down upon us we were all clapping like we do in Charismatic circles.

Jesus said something that astounded me. Understand

99

what I'm going to say so you don't get the wrong impression about it. He said to me, "Clapping is neither praise nor worship." *Jesus* said that to me. He went on to say, "To clap is to applaud."

I'd never heard anyone say that. And even though I had been troubled at times when the congregation clapped so much during an inspired utterance that the anointing lifted and we missed some things the Spirit of God wanted to get over to us, these words of Jesus almost shocked me.

But as He continued to speak, I began to understand why I had been troubled. Best of all, I began to see what could be done to cooperate with Him so the fullness of His blessing and the depth of the move of the Spirit could come upon the Church.

A Help or a Hindrance?

In order to gain a better understanding of the place clapping should have in our services, first of all we need to understand what clapping is. Jesus said clapping is applause. He said it is neither praise nor worship. Well, if it isn't praise and it isn't worship, where does it fit in *at all* in our services?

I got a little illustration some time after Campmeeting that helped my understanding of clapping and I want to share it with you.

When a little boy receives a birthday present from his daddy, he may clap his hands and jump up and down. But he is not praising or worshipping his daddy — he is expressing his own excitement and rejoicing over what he has just received. In other words, his clapping is only for his own benefit. It's an outworking of his own emotions.

In our services, we may clap sometimes just because we're excited or we're rejoicing, but that's not praising or worshipping God.

In the visitation, Jesus discussed clapping with me from the Scriptures. He said, "There is not one scripture in the New Testament about clapping. The Bible says in Psalm 47:1: *'O clap your hands, all ye people; shout unto God with the voice of triumph.'* Clapping in this verse denoted an attitude of victory; it was not a form of praise. That is the only time clapping before the Lord is mentioned, and that is in the Old Testament. There are also some occurrences in the Old Testament where people clapped their hands for other reasons, but it had no connection with the worship of God. Then there are also scriptures about the waves and the floods clapping their hands, but you understand, that is figurative language.

"There is not one single scripture," Jesus said to me, "in the New Covenant about anyone clapping their hands."

We do, however, have New Testament scripture for lifting our hands in worship to the Lord. In fact, the only instruction we have in the New Testament about what we are to do with our hands, is to lift them up! You remember, Paul — or as I like to say — the Holy Spirit through Paul, said, *"I will therefore that men pray every where, lifting up holy hands, without wrath and doubting"* (1 Tim. 2:8).

We've all heard it said that praise is the highest form of prayer. You see, prayer is not what many people think it is. Prayer isn't "Gimme, gimme, gimme." Among other things, prayer is fellowshipping with God. One type of prayer is praise and worship. Therefore, we would do no injustice to the text to read First Timothy 2:8 like this: *"I will therefore that men . . .* [praise] *every where, lifting up holy hands. . . . "*

You see, the world claps or applauds, but you do not see them lifting their hands to praise or celebrate. No, the Church of the Lord Jesus Christ is to lift up holy hands to praise the Lord!

"The world claps," Jesus said to me. "Saints praise."

Then He illustrated it something like this: You can walk by dark dives (night clubs, beer joints, etc.) and look inside at what is going on. Those inside may be watching a show with nude dancers, and you will see them clapping their hands. They may be watching a sports event on a screen, and you will see them clapping their hands. Or you can go to a political rally, and when the politician says something everyone likes, they will clap their hands. But in none of these places do you see the crowd lift their hands.

Now that doesn't mean clapping is wrong in itself. But we do need to distinguish between clapping which is a natural expression of this world, and the raising of our hands which is a scriptural expression of the realm to which we as believers belong. We also need to identify when to clap and when to lift our hands in praise. Clapping at the wrong time can cause the anointing to lift from a service.

For example, many times when the Spirit of God is moving in a service through tongues and interpretation or prophecy, everyone will start clapping right in the middle of the interpretation or the prophecy. People get excited and clap, but their clapping prevents everyone present from hearing what the Holy Spirit wanted to say. Such clapping couldn't be done in the Spirit, for if the tongue and interpretation or the prophecy is by the unction

of the Spirit, then the Holy Spirit is interrupting Himself.
If the Holy Spirit is saying something to the church and
no one can hear it, then we're either wasting our time by
allowing the manifestation of the Spirit or we're wasting
our time by clapping.

Is prophecy right, or is it not? Is the Holy Spirit saying
something, or is He not? Would the Holy Spirit interrupt
Himself? Would people be moved upon by the Holy Spirit
to clap when the Holy Spirit is saying something? No,
we've just gotten "clap happy" in Charismatic circles, and
it grieves the Holy Spirit.

As a minister, I've been in the position of being the
one used by God to speak forth in prophecy or interpretation of tongues — when right in the middle of the prophecy,
everyone will start clapping. Unless I am very careful, I
can lose the anointing because the clapping distracts me,
making it difficult to hear what the Holy Spirit is saying.

And then there have been times when the anointing
left in spite of my efforts to stay in the flow of the Spirit,
because the Holy Spirit was grieved. Clapping in the midst
of the Spirit's manifestation displays irreverence for Him.

On several occasions, I have known there was more the
Spirit wanted to say and I've known it was important that
we hear the entire message. But what can you do? You
can't continue without His help.

Even if the anointing does not lift and I continue
to speak, no one can hear what is being said. If it's not
for people to hear, why would the Holy Spirit move upon
me to speak?

At other times, I've been up preaching under the
anointing — I mean just going after it — when everyone
started clapping in response to something I said. Well,

they're applauding to show their agreement with what I said, but that is not the time or the place for applause. In the first place, I can't go on preaching because everyone will miss what I say while the clapping is going on. If what you're saying is by the unction of the Spirit, people need to hear it. And there should be enough respect for the Holy Spirit not to interrupt Him when He's moving.

Even during our worship, clapping is often done at inappropriate times. It causes the anointing to lift and destroys that sweet closeness of His Presence that we all sense.

You can see how this could happen even in a natural relationship such as the relationship between a man and a woman. What if the man and woman were sitting together talking for some time, exchanging words of endearment, and suddenly one of them began to clap? Wouldn't that seem inappropriate? Friends, when we're praising and worshipping the Lord, *He* is present!

For a long time in Charismatic circles, we've had the habit of clapping after every song we sing during a time of praise and worship. Possibly this has occurred because people have felt a need to respond in some way but haven't known exactly how to respond. However, clapping after every song disrupts the flow of worship. It takes our attention off the Lord. How much better it would be to lift our hands in worship and speak forth our thanksgiving and adoration to Him who first loved us!

When To Clap and When To Praise

Don't misunderstand me; it's all right to clap in church services under some circumstances. Some folks have accused me of saying that we should never clap at all. That is *not* what I have said, and that's not what Jesus said to me.

During His visitation with me, the main thing the Lord was trying to say about clapping was to correct the excessive clapping that is taking place in our churches today. Instead of putting clapping *before* the lifting of our hands or the praising of God with our lips, it should come *last*, if at all. And it should be regulated — it should be at a minimum in services and not at a maximum.

Therefore, we need to understand when clapping is appropriate and when it is inappropriate.

If the congregation is singing an up-tempo song, it's all right for folks to clap their hands in time with the music. But when the song ends and the worship leader asks people to praise the Lord, they should lift their hands to praise Him as the New Testament teaches.

Also, in church, we shouldn't be applauding singers when they minister in special music. Their talent is God-given and is to be used for the glory and praise of God. They're not putting on a performance (or at least they shouldn't be); they're ministering in music to encourage the congregation to get their eyes on God and to lift them up into His Presence. If we appreciate their music, we should lift our hands and praise God. Applauding singers is not praising God, and we are to praise God. We are to lift up holy hands in praise of God. Now don't get upset if you've been clapping at the wrong times. I've been just as guilty as anyone else, so don't take exception to what I am saying.

There are times when we applaud a speaker to let him know we're glad he's come. It is a gesture of welcome after he has been introduced, and it's strictly on a natural level. That's all right as long as it's not overdone. We're not worshipping or praising the speaker.

However, since Jesus' visitation to me, I've been giving a lot of thought to things I hadn't really considered too much before. I have some compunction now about saying, "Let's all give God a hand." I don't think we can give God a hand like we would the President of the United States. I don't think we should give God a "clap-offering."

Paul said to the Corinthians in First Corinthians 2:3, *"And I was with you . . . in fear. . . ."* That doesn't mean he was afraid of something like someone would be afraid of a storm or a rattlesnake. That means he had a respect, an awareness of the awesomeness of God and of his responsibilities as a minister of God.

The Hebrew scribes who copied the Scriptures by hand had such a respect for God that before they would write His Name they would stop and take a ritual bath and put on clean clothes.

We've gotten away from the respect for God that we should have. I don't feel comfortable giving God a hand like you would a politician; I don't want to bring Him down on a level with man. He is high and holy. The New Testament teaches us to lift our hands and our voices to God in praise.

Jesus said to me, "Pastors should teach their congregations little by little about the move of the Holy Spirit so they'll know how to move with Him and they'll know when to keep quiet. They shouldn't scold their people or train them in a negative way, but they need to teach them to be quiet when the Holy Spirit is in manifestation. They should tell them to listen, and after the Holy Spirit has spoken, to lift their hands and praise Me."

Reverence

As Jesus was discussing the subject of clapping and raising of the hands in praise to Him, He made this statement: "When you really learn to praise and worship Me in the right way, you'll find a stronger anointing and a greater move of the Holy Spirit in your midst."

We need to learn that when the Presence of the Lord is in a place, we should not dissipate that Presence — that power. Be quiet and reverent and then you'll see the manifestation of the Holy Ghost that your heart has longed for.

You haven't see anything like what we will see when the Body of Christ gets to that place of worship.

We were in that kind of atmosphere worshipping God in one of our crusades, and there were five people sitting in wheelchairs. Three of them just got up and walked off. No one laid a hand on them. But for that to happen, we have to begin to get into the flow of the Holy Spirit.

When you get in an atmosphere of true worship, and God begins to move by His Spirit, you can just reach out and take what belongs to you in Christ. The Bible teaches laying on of hands, but you really don't have to have hands laid on you when the Presence of God is so strongly in manifestation. No matter what you may need, you can reach out and take it and say, "It's mine!"

But when people begin to demonstrate in the flesh, the anointing lifts — it flies away like a bird taking flight because it grieves the Spirit. I wish I could get that over to people. I've been in meetings of several thousand where the Holy Spirit was moving, and suddenly, I knew by the Holy Spirit when the anointing came upon me to stand over in the office of the prophet and minister to the people. I was just ready to call out certain people, to point to them right where they stood, and say, "The Spirit of God just showed me this is what is wrong with you." I've ministered that way many times through the years, and every time, the people have been healed. When I've ministered under that kind of an anointing, I've never had one person fail to get healed. I could tell you about thousands of people who were healed that way through the many years of my ministry.

However, sometimes when the anointing has come to minister in that office, people in the congregation have gotten up and started moving about. The lack of reverence for God moving in the service grieved the Spirit and He left; the anointing lifted from me. I mean, just like a bird sitting on your shoulder, it flew away — the anointing left. And those people didn't even know it; they went out talking and whispering. Maybe they were in a hurry to leave and get something to eat, but they didn't know that they had just hindered some dear sick people from being healed — sometimes people with terminal cases.

I got a note from one pastor who told me about a woman in one of his services who had a terminal illness. The doctor said she had terminal cancer and had ninety days to live. The pastor wrote that the Lord healed her in one of his services. A terminal case like that healed because the Spirit of God moved supernaturally! However, then in the service so many in the congregation began to talk and move about that it grieved the Spirit of God and He stopped moving. You can't help people then because

it's the anointing that breaks the yoke. *The Bible said,*
it is the anointing that breaks the yoke. *".. . the yoke shall
be destroyed because of the anointing"* (Isa. 10:27).

There is a move of the Spirit of God that God is wanting in this day. God is wanting to do something for us
today! Let's not hinder Him. Let's just cooperate with
Him and let's be reverent. When God is moving, let's just
sit quietly and reverence him. Then if we want to shout
afterwards — we can shout. I mean, afterwards, *when the
crippled start dancing in the Spirit,* that's the time to jump
up and dance with them!

God has been trying to teach us some of these things,
and we've been endeavoring to demonstrate them for
several years.

I was preaching down in East Texas a number of years
ago in a Full Gospel church, and God instructed me to lay
hands on people to be filled with the Holy Spirit. Laying
hands on people to receive the Holy Spirit is *God's plan* —
it's Biblical.

However, in Texas in 1950, people didn't do that. But
the Lord told me to do it. I went to a little Full Gospel
church, and I just set out to do what God told me to do.
I called for those who wanted to be filled with the Spirit
to come forward, and seven people came to the altar.

I purposely had them sit down on the altar, because
I wanted to teach them a little first. I knew if I didn't teach
them, they would just start praying at the altar and get
themselves in a rut *tarrying* for God, trying to receive the
Holy Spirit because they'd been doing that for years. (I
ran into one fellow who had been seeking to be baptized
in the Holy Spirit for fifty years.) So I knew if I just had
them come down to the altar and pray, they'd get in that

same rut and not be able to get out of it. I purposely kept them off their knees, so I could give them a little instruction first.

I taught them for a while, and then I laid hands on the first one and he immediately began to speak in tongues. When that happened, the people in the congregation jumped up and started shouting and running everywhere. I had to go back to the pulpit and shout in order to get their attention so they could hear me. I said, "Wait a minute, wait. WAIT! WAIT! Sit down." They all sat down. Then I told them, "Now wait, don't dissipate the power by shouting and carrying on. We've got six more people here that need to be filled with the Spirit. Let's get them filled; then we'll all shout and demonstrate if we want to." They looked at me like a cow at a new gate; that was all new to them.

I went down the line laying hands on those other six people, and every single one of them was filled with the Holy Spirit and started speaking with tongues. When the last one was filled with the Holy Spirit, I started speaking in tongues and just turned around and ran down the aisle, ran back up another aisle, ran up on the platform, danced a little jig for joy, and ran back down the aisle again. Everyone just sat there and looked at me.

Finally, I had to say to them, "It's time to dance now." They hadn't gotten their timing right! I told them, "After seven people get filled with the Holy Spirit, it's time to run and dance!" But, see, a lot of people want to run and dance at the other fellow's expense — when the timing's wrong — and dissipate the power.

During this visitation before Campmeeting '87, the Lord dealt with me very strongly about the fact that He's trying to get the Body of Christ to the place where He can move by His Spirit in our midst. I'm gradually seeing that come to pass. The Body of Christ is finally coming to the place where God can move in our services like He wants to. This is the time! The Body of Christ has finally come to that time now, and is getting ready for the move that God wants in the earth, glory to God!

Several years ago, the Lord said to me, "There is a move of the Spirit of God that will be lost to this present generation unless they are taught and led into it."

I don't know that we have been successful at this yet. But we're finally coming to the place where we can begin to teach this.

The Lord went on to say to me, "Some of the old-time Pentecostals knew something about that deeper move of the Spirit. The modern-day Pentecostals — this new generation of Charismatics — know little or nothing about it. Charismatics know little or nothing about the move of My Spirit. Charismatics know a little about praising Me, but they know nothing at all about true worship."

You see, when you talk about worship, there is a spirit of reverence that goes along with it. As I've already mentioned, in the church I pastored in Farmersville, Texas, we regularly experienced the awesome Presence of God. But we were always very careful to reverence the Holy Spirit in our services. Consequently, the miraculous was an everyday occurrence with us. We haven't really experienced that in the Charismatic Movement. There's been a lightness in Charismatic services; a "hip-hip-hooray" type of atmosphere.

Ohhhh! But in times past, I've seen the Presence of God come in and fill the temple! When I say "the temple,"

I mean a body of believers. During those times when the Presence of God came into our services, no one moved; an awesome Presence filled the room. I wish I could describe that awesome Presence to you. Some things are just too reverent to talk about and it's hard to find words to describe them. But I've seen the awesome Presence of God come in and fill the temple. I long to see the Body of Christ experience that Presence on a continual basis!

At this writing, it has been almost a year since Jesus' 1987 visitation with me. In our own ministry, we have been experiencing the deeper move of the Spirit of God among us which Jesus promised. Just a short while after the summer Campmeeting, our crusade team was in Detroit. One of our singers was singing a song of the Spirit, fresh from heaven, given by the inspiration of the Spirit in that moment. Upon hearing one of the lines of the song, the crowd began to clap. The singer stopped and exhorted the congregation, "Please don't clap anymore." They received the instruction and listened to what the Spirit was saying as he went on with the spiritual song.

A depth, an indescribable Presence like a cloud filled the auditorium. We had no preaching that night. The Holy Spirit came upon me in a greater measure to minister by the Spirit in healings and in other ways.

Afterwards, I asked those seated in the ministers' section if they had noticed how the anointing increased after we stopped clapping and turned our attention and worship to God. They all indicated by nodding their heads that they had.

There is a reverence, an awesome sense of the holiness of God which can come upon a congregation. As the Body of Christ, we've got to get back to that place of reverence.

For when we reverence God and give Him the honor and worship due unto Him, His Presence will fill the place where we are gathered. It is His Presence which will meet the deepest longings of our hearts and set the captives free.

Chapter 9
Be Being Filled — Speaking

Following our 1987 Campmeeting, someone asked me, "What did Jesus emphasize the most during His three-hour visitation with you?"

Without question, what Jesus emphasized most is what we will be discussing in this chapter.

Jesus said to me, "My plan under the New Covenant is for every believer to be filled with the Holy Spirit."

As we've pointed out already, every believer or follower of God in the Old Testament was not filled with the Holy Spirit. Only the prophet, priest, king, and those called to do a special work for God had the anointing of the Spirit. And that anointing only came *upon* them; it did not dwell *within* them. In the Old Testament those we would call "laymen" did not have the Spirit of God within them or upon them. That's one reason the New Covenant is a better Covenant — it provides a way for every person who is born again to have God's Spirit actually residing on the inside of them.

In our own individual lives, the New Testament emphasizes being filled with the Spirit. Jesus directed me to Ephesians 5:18,19 which I knew well. He discussed with me in detail everything I have included in this chapter.

In the Old Testament, God's people were strictly worshipping Him *in the flesh*. Only the king, the priest, and the prophet had the Holy Spirit upon them. The rest of them didn't have the Holy Spirit *on* them, or *in* them, so their display of worship was a natural display, done in the flesh.

However, in the New Testament, the emphasis for

worship is that it is to be done *in the Spirit.* That's why
the Bible says we are to be filled with the Spirit. Let's
notice what Paul said, or as I like to say it, let's see what
the Holy Spirit said through the Apostle Paul.

EPHESIANS 5:18
18 And be not drunk with wine, wherein is excess; but be
filled with the Spirit.

This verse can be read like this: "Don't be drunk on
wine; be drunk on the *Spirit.* " Have you ever been drunk
on the Spirit? You can be so filled with the Spirit that you
stagger around like a drunk man. Be filled with the Spirit.
Now notice what they did when they were filled with the
Spirit: They began to speak with other tongues. The New
Testament puts emphasis on being filled with the Holy
Spirit and *speaking* with other tongues.

ACTS 2:1-4
1   And when the day of Pentecost was fully come, they
were all with one accord in one place.
2   And suddenly there came a sound from heaven as of
a rushing mighty wind, and it filled all the house where
they were sitting.
3   And there appeared unto them cloven tongues like as
of fire, and it sat upon each of them.
4   And they were ALL FILLED WITH THE HOLY
GHOST, AND BEGAN TO SPEAK with other tongues,
as the Spirit gave them utterance.

We can also see the Bible emphasis of being filled with
the Spirit and speaking in other tongues ten years later.
An angel appeared to Cornelius and told him to send men
to Joppa to inquire in the house of Simon the Tanner for
Peter. Proceeding with the men to Cornelius' house, Peter

began to preach to those gathered there.

ACTS 10:44-46
44 While Peter yet spake these words, the Holy Ghost fell
on all them which heard the word.
45 And they of the circumcision which believed were
astonished . . . because that ON THE Gentiles ALSO WAS
POURED OUT THE GIFT OF THE HOLY GHOST.
46 FOR THEY HEARD THEM SPEAK with tongues,
and magnify God.

We see this again in Acts chapter 19, when Paul laid
his hands on believers in Ephesus.

ACTS 19:1-6
1 And it came to pass, that . . . Paul having passed
through the upper coasts came to Ephesus: and finding
certain disciples,
2 He said unto them, Have ye received the Holy Ghost
since ye believed? And they said . . . We have not so much
as heard whether there be any Holy Ghost.
3 And he said unto them, Unto what then were ye
baptized? And they said, Unto John's baptism.
4 Then said Paul, John verily baptized with the baptism
of repentance, saying unto the people, that they should
believe on him which should come after him, that is, on
Christ Jesus.
5 When they heard this, they were baptized in the name
of the Lord Jesus.
6 And when Paul had laid his hands upon them, THE
HOLY GHOST CAME ON THEM; AND THEY SPAKE
with tongues. . . .

The Bible says that when hands were laid on these
disciples, they spoke in other tongues. When hands are
laid on you to receive the Holy Spirit, you can do
something other than what the Bible says to do and it will

grieve the Holy Spirit. The Bible says we are *to speak in tongues.*

For example, when the Holy Spirit comes upon you, you can just start shouting in English and not speak in tongues at all, and you'll shout the power off of you. Shouting is all right in its place, but when hands are laid on you to receive the Holy Spirit, that's the wrong time to shout. No, yield to the Holy Spirit and begin to speak in tongues.

In all of these New Testament accounts, the people spoke with tongues after the Holy Ghost came upon them. Did you notice that? Being filled with the Holy Spirit and speaking is the New Testament pattern.

> **EPHESIANS 5:18,19**
> 18 And be not drunk with wine, wherein is excess; BUT BE FILLED WITH THE SPIRIT;
> 19 SPEAKING to yourselves in psalms and hymns and spiritual songs, singing and making melody in your heart to the Lord.

Notice the key words in this passage: *". . . be filled with the Spirit; speaking. . ."* (vv. 18,19).

The Ephesians were one of the groups of people who had already received the initial infilling of the Holy Spirit under Paul's ministry (Acts 19:1-6). Yet he writes them in Ephesians 5:18,19, and tells them again to be filled with the Spirit. Why did he say that to them? Weren't they already filled with the Holy Spirit? Before I comment on that, let me say this.

I've still got every Bible I ever had, and in every one of them, you can readily see where they are worn the most — over in the Epistles. Why? Those are the letters that were written to me! The four gospels were not written TO me, they were written FOR me. The Old Testament was not written TO me, it was written FOR me. Do you understand the difference?

Every single Epistle was written *to* you and *to* me! They're written *to* believers — *to* the Church! They're written *to* the Christian. The Epistles are where I've lived all these years. I want to find out what God is writing to the Church, and what He is saying to me! I'm not so concerned about what He said to the Jews. I'm primarily concerned about what He's saying to me!

In the Epistles, we find out that the New Testament emphasizes being filled with the Spirit.

In writing to the Ephesian Christians who had already been filled initially with the Holy Spirit in Acts 19, Paul exhorted them again in Ephesians 5 to be *filled* with the Spirit. At first reading, this might seem confusing. However, what Paul had reference to in Ephesians 5:18 went beyond the initial infilling of the Holy Spirit and speaking with tongues which the Ephesians had received when he laid hands upon them in Acts 19:1-6.

Greek scholars tell us that the literal translation of Ephesians 5:18, ". . . be filled with the Spirit," actually contains a play on words. It literally reads, ". . . be *being* filled with the Spirit." Paul was encouraging these Ephesians to *continue* speaking with tongues in order to stay filled up with the Holy Spirit. In other words, they needed to have a constant infilling of the Spirit — a continual experience of being filled with the Spirit and speaking forth in supernatural utterance in order to stay filled with the Spirit.

I want you to notice that Paul was writing to the whole

church at Ephesus — he wasn't writing just to preachers. It is God's plan for *every* believer, every Christian, living under the New Covenant to be continually filled with the Holy Spirit and to worship in the Spirit. The way we *maintain* a continual infilling and maintain our walk in the Spirit is through speaking divinely inspired utterances to the Lord. This is one form of New Testament worship.

These divinely inspired utterances can have several different means of expression. One means of expression is to magnify and worship God in other tongues, as we've already seen that the saints did in Acts 10:46: *"For they heard them speak with tongues, and MAGNIFY God...."* However, Paul went on to mention several other expressions in Ephesians 5:19.

Psalms, Hymns, and Spiritual Songs

Pay close attention to the following two scriptures. Notice how the believer's utterances inspired by the Holy Spirit ascend in worship *"to the Lord."*

EPHESIANS 5:18,19
18 ... but be filled with the Spirit;
19 Speaking to yourselves in psalms and hymns and spiritual songs, SINGING AND MAKING MELODY IN YOUR HEART TO THE LORD.

Colossians 3:16 is a companion scripture to Ephesians 5:18,19. It too emphasizes worship unto the Lord.

COLOSSIANS 3:16
16 Let the word of Christ dwell in you richly in all wisdom; teaching and admonishing one another in psalms and

hymns and spiritual songs, SINGING WITH GRACE IN YOUR HEARTS TO THE LORD.

Paul was speaking to every believer when he said that we are to speak to ourselves in psalms, hymns, and spiritual songs. We are to speak to *ourselves*. This is something we are to do in our own personal, private life in communion with God.

A *psalm* is a spiritual poem or ode. It may rhyme or it may not; however, there is an element of poetry about it. It may be sung, chanted, or just recited.

The Old Testament records 150 psalms. In fact, the Book of Psalms was Israel's prayer and songbook. Many of the Psalms were written by David, who had the Holy Spirit upon him, and they tell us what was happening to him — the tests and the trials he was going through when that psalm was given to him. Though some were given to him for his own special benefit, they bless us because they are Spirit-anointed and because we may be going through a similar experience.

I speak in psalms quite frequently. A psalm may be sung or it may be chanted or just recited. A person given to music would naturally sing a psalm given by the Spirit. The same psalm that I would just speak out, someone who is given to music would sing. I'm not a singer; I don't have a voice for singing, so I just speak out the psalms the Holy Spirit gives me.

Believe it or not, I took voice lessons. Finally, the voice teacher said to me, "I've never said this to anyone in all my years of teaching, but I believe if I were you, I wouldn't take any more lessons." I never could get any higher than a certain note. Singing is not my forte; I've got to leave that to others. I can make a joyful noise and that's about it. So I speak in psalms.

Many times, God will give you a psalm in your private prayer life just for your own benefit. On the other hand, a hymn is a song of praise and worship addressed to and directed toward God.

A *spiritual song* is a song that brings forth the revelation of the Word that the Holy Spirit has given you.

"Let the word of Christ dwell in you richly . . ." (Col. 3:16). That doesn't necessarily mean just the written Word. They didn't have a written New Testament then. The Bible is talking about the Word that the Holy Ghost brings to you. It may be a scripture, a word of encouragement, or a word of exhortation, etc.

So many have read Ephesians 5:19 and Colossians 3:16 and have tried to interpret these scriptures in the light of our Western culture. They have thought this meant singing out of a songbook, or hymnal. However, it couldn't mean that because when Paul wrote these letters, they didn't have printing presses!

And although there are many good songs which were probably inspired by the Holy Spirit, most songs in our songbooks are embalmed with unbelief.

However, psalms, hymns, and spiritual songs are given by the Holy Spirit — they're "hot off the wire" from heaven. And they are scriptural, because anything the Holy Ghost gives is scriptural.

Jesus called this kind of utterance, New Testament worship. And true worship must be *"in spirit and in truth"* (John 4:23).

Once we are initially filled with the Spirit and speak supernaturally, we are to *continue* speaking supernaturally.

The Word of God in Ephesians 5:18,19 and Colossians 3:16 is talking about the supernatural utterance the Holy Ghost gives you on the spur of the moment by the spirit of prophecy. One of the manifestations of the Holy Spirit is prophecy (1 Cor. 12:10).

What is prophecy?

It is inspired utterance in a *known* tongue. The simple gift of prophecy ". . . *speaketh unto men to edification, and exhortation, and comfort"* (1 Cor. 14:3). It is <u>not</u> to be confused with the prophet's office which often gives revelation of the future.

First Corinthians 14:31 says, *"For ye may all prophesy. . . ."* In other words, all believers ought to be prophesying. Every single believer ought to be speaking to himself in psalms, hymns, and spiritual songs in his private devotional life.

That is part of the operation of the gift of prophecy. (Folks think they are not prophesying unless they get up in church and give a public utterance. Oh, no, that is just a minor part of this manifestation.)

I speak in psalms in my personal prayer life all the time. Many times for an hour or two in the nighttime, I speak to myself in psalms. Sometimes I speak to myself in psalms nearly all night long.

Speaking in psalms, hymns, and spiritual songs can also be done in public assembly if opportunity is given. Let's look again at Colossians 3:16:

COLOSSIANS 3:16
16 Let the word of Christ dwell in you richly in all wisdom; TEACHING AND ADMONISHING ONE ANOTHER in psalms and hymns and spiritual songs, singing with grace in your hearts to the Lord.

You see, psalms, hymns, and spiritual songs can be used in public assembly to teach and admonish one another.

Now consider what Paul wrote to the church at Corinth. "*. . . when ye come together* [talking about a believers' meeting] *EVERY ONE of you hath a psalm . . .*" (1 Cor. 14:26). How many of you? Every one!

The reason everyone in the Early Church could have a psalm when they came together was because they had been speaking in psalms in their own private prayer lives at home.

The benefits of speaking to ourselves in psalms, hymns, and spiritual songs are great.

First, it enables us to have true communion with God and to worship Him in Spirit and in truth. It is also a means of spiritual edification — we stay encouraged and built up in the Lord. Finally, it is a means of keeping us separated from the world. It causes us to be conscious of His indwelling Presence, and if we're conscious that He is living in us, it is bound to affect the way we live.

It is God's plan that we be filled with His Spirit and speak forth in psalms, hymns, and spiritual songs. But some may say, "I don't know how to do that. I've never done it before! How can I enter into that kind of walk in the Spirit?"

Stir Up the Gift

Many believers have been filled with the Holy Ghost and have spoken in other tongues, yet they've never spoken in tongues again since their initial infilling. They were once filled, but they've not maintained a fresh experience with God. They haven't obeyed the injunction of Ephesians 5:18, "... *be* [being] *filled with the Spirit.*"

I've had people say to me, "Well, I don't know whether I can speak with tongues again or not." But the Holy Spirit is still inside you, and He's the one who gives you the utterance. All you need to do is expect Him to give you utterance and then yield to Him. In other words, stir up the gift of God within you!

Notice what the Scripture says about this — not what man says, not what people think. Paul, in writing to Timothy, said:

> **2 TIMOTHY 1:6**
> 6 Wherefore I put thee in remembrance that thou STIR UP THE GIFT OF GOD, which is in thee by the putting on of my hands.

What "gift" of God was Paul talking about? There is a twofold application of this verse. The word "gift" in this verse can refer to impartations by the Holy Spirit given when God sets people aside for service. For example, in Acts 13:2, the Bible says, "*As they ministered to the Lord, and fasted, the Holy Ghost said, Separate me Barnabas and Saul for the work whereunto I have called them.*" Something was imparted to Barnabas and Saul by the Holy Spirit as they were set apart for service.

We can also see this when Timothy was set apart for ministry.

> **1 TIMOTHY 4:14**
> 14 Neglect not the gift that is in thee, which was given thee by prophecy, with the laying on of the hands of the presbytery.

The second application of this verse is that the *gift* Timothy received when Paul laid his hands on him was the gift of the Holy Spirit. We know from the Scriptures that Paul laid his hands on many people and they received the Holy Spirit.

Notice what Paul said Timothy was to do with this gift in Second Timothy 1:6. He said, "Stir up the gift of God that is within you"! You are to stir up the Holy Spirit on the inside of you!

You can stir up the Holy Spirit *yourself* within your own spirit by praying in other tongues. After you pray in other tongues awhile, then you can begin to speak to yourself ". . . *in psalms and hymns and spiritual songs, singing and making melody in your heart to the Lord*" (Eph. 5:19). That is how you enter into New Testament worship.

If speaking to ourselves in psalms, hymns, and spiritual songs is God's plan for believers living under the New Covenant, then should we not determine to pursue that plan?

I want to live a life pleasing to God; I want to flow with His plan — not my own. And I want to enter into the fullness of all that He has for me, don't you? He has told us how we can do it, and I, for one, intend to obey God!

Chapter 10
Demonstration of the Spirit

When Jesus stood with me above the Tulsa Convention Center and talked about His plan for believers living under the New Testament, He turned to me and said, "Demonstrate to the people. After you teach, say to the people, 'I'm to teach you not only by precept, but by example.' It is scriptural to follow godly examples."

He then directed me to the following scripture and showed me how my interpretation of it had not been exact.

1 CORINTHIANS 2:4
4 And my speech and my preaching was not with enticing words of man's wisdom, but in demonstration of the Spirit and of power.

Notice how Paul said that: *". . . my speech and my preaching was . . . in demonstration of the Spirit and of power."* Not demonstration *of* power and the Spirit, but demonstration *of the Spirit* AND of power. The demonstrations *of power* are the power gifts in manifestation: Special faith, working of miracles, and gifts of healings.

However, the Holy Spirit also works and demonstrates in the revelation gifts and in the utterance gifts. Paul is saying, "I preach in demonstration of the Spirit."

So Paul is really saying two things in this verse: 1) I come in demonstration *of power,* and 2) I come in *demonstration* of the *Spirit.*

The demonstration *of power* refers to the power gifts in manifestation: Special faith, working of miracles, gifts of healings. Those gifts demonstrate the *power* of the Holy Spirit — that's why they are called "power gifts."

127

But Paul also said, "I preach in demonstration of the Spirit." The Holy Spirit further *demonstrates* Himself, for example, in the revelation gifts and in the gifts of utterance.

We've thought that "preaching in demonstration of the Spirit and of power," was referring only to preaching with the power gifts in operation, or preaching with what we'd call "signs and wonders" with miraculous healings taking place. But, no, this scripture also refers to the way the Spirit *demonstrates* or *manifests* Himself.

We could say then, that the Holy Spirit *demonstrates* Himself: 1) in the power gifts, 2) in the utterance and revelation gifts, and 3) He manifests Himself in demonstration *through* the ministry gifts.

God wants to bring us to the place where we *demonstrate* the Holy Spirit *and* we demonstrate the *power* of the Holy Spirit.

We can all be involved in demonstrations of the Spirit by prophecy because the Bible says we can all exercise the simple gift of prophecy: "... *ye may all prophesy one by one* ..." (1 Cor. 14:31). Another scripture that tells us we can all be involved in demonstration of the Spirit through prophecy is found in Ephesians 5:18,19: "... *be not drunk with wine, wherein is excess; but be filled with the Spirit; SPEAKING to yourselves* ..." (Eph. 5:18,19). As we have seen, speaking to ourselves in psalms and hymns and spiritual songs is an operation of the simple gift of prophecy or supernatural utterance. So prophecy is also a "demonstration *of the Spirit.*"

In that visitation with Jesus, I saw us *demonstrating* the Holy Spirit. In that visitation, Jesus not only told me to *demonstrate,* but then I saw us doing it. In the actual

Campmeeting service, I only acted out what I had already seen.

As I stood with Jesus and looked down through the roof of the Tulsa Convention Center onto the Monday night service of Campmeeting, I saw myself demonstrating speaking in psalms. I didn't hear what the psalms were until I was actually in that evening service. I also saw others of our ministry team, whom I recognized, demonstrating the Spirit in psalms, hymns, and spiritual songs. Then during the actual service, everything happened just as I had seen.

The following are some psalms which I spoke out in that Campmeeting service as they came by the Spirit. The other people I had seen demonstrating the Spirit were more given to music; therefore, they sang what was given to them by the Holy Spirit.

To help those who have never spoken in psalms, I will try to explain how psalms come to me: I feel, or sense, a psalm as it comes up out of my spirit — out of the inside of me. Usually, I just get the title, although sometimes the first word or two comes. I have never gotten more than two lines. Beyond that, I do not know what I am going to say. If I am in a public assembly and the unction is not there, then I'm lost.

It takes faith to speak in psalms. The whole Christian life is a faith walk, for without faith, it is impossible to please God. If He gave you the whole psalm at once, you'd be walking by sight and you couldn't please Him by reciting it.

After I speak whatever I have in faith, the rest comes by the spirit of prophecy. I get over into the flow of it.

I'm sure many Christians have had this happen to them

in their personal devotions and didn't know what it was,
so they didn't yield to it!

The following psalms came as I taught in demonstration of the Spirit. When I began to speak, I had just one word which was the title for each psalm. The rest rose up from within my spirit as I continued to speak forth in faith.

YESTERDAY

Yesterday is gone and should be forgotten.
Satan will oftentime (as well as friends)
   remind you of your yesterdays.
But remember that your yesterdays — all that is wrong —
   is under the blood.
And all that is good and is right,
   it will be all right for you to recite.
But walk in the light and know
   that your yesterdays are forever gone.
And today is beautiful.
So walk with the Lord and enjoy His blessings.
For yesterday does not exist.

TODAY

Today is not as dark
   as some men would have you believe.
Today is not as desolate and desperate
   as the media ofttime would portray.

Today is the day of the Lord —
   a day of deliverance,
   a day of blessing,
   a day of visitation.

For, you see, those who walk with the Lord

walk in the light.
And they walk by faith and not by sight.

But those who walk in darkness cannot see.
Yea, even the god of this world
   has darkened their minds,
   and all they see is desolation, darkness,
   and the end of time.

The end of time will surely come.
But, remember, the Master said to us
   who walk and live in this clime,
"When these things begin to come to pass,
   lift up your heads and look up!
Rejoice! for your redemption draweth nigh!"

So today is not dark;
Today is bright, and today is light.
Walk in the light and all of your pathways
   will forever be bright.

TOMORROW

So many are worried and depressed
   and some even almost driven to suicide —
   frustrated about tomorrow.

What will tomorrow bring?
Will tomorrow ever come?
What about tomorrow?
Will I be here?

What about tomorrow?
Will it bring fame or will it bring fortune?
Will it bring blessing?

Will it be bad or will it be good?

Yea, saith the Lord of hosts,
  tomorrow belongs unto the saints.
Tomorrow *can* be filled,
  and will be filled with victory
  even as today — when you walk by faith.

So see tomorrow as a stepping stone
  to greater success and achievement
  in the realm of God.
Tomorrow is bright,
  for tomorrow belongs to the saints
  who walk in the light.

Tomorrow is good, for the Father of lights
  sendeth down always unto His own
  that which is good.
For God is good; Yea, His mercy endureth forever.

So do not feel any anxiety about tomorrow.
Trust in the Lord and leave it in His hands.
Walk by faith and shout above the turmoil.
All is right and all is bright
  for we are children of light.

Darkness and gloom will overtake any
  who will yield unto Satan
  and walk in his way.
Darkness and gloom; negativism and doubt.
Fear, you see, dominates those
  who do not know what it is all about.

But those who are enlightened by His Word,
  knoweth that the trial of their faith

is more precious than gold.

So in the midst of the trial
and in the midst of the test
they sound forth the shout of victory and rejoice.
For they know that victory
belongs unto the children of God.

They know that there came out from heaven long ago
the Champion sent by the Father
to those who live down here below.

And in the world of darkness, He came and said,
"I am the Light of the world.
Follow Me and you will walk not in darkness."

So darkness and gloom
are a thing of the past.
For now you are the light of the world.
Yea, now you walk in the fullness of God
and the glory of the Father.

And all that He has provided is thine.
So shout it above all the roar of the enemy.
Because, you see, all that God has said
and declared is sublime.

VICTORY

Victory is not in places and things.
Victory is not in people and man's plan.
Victory is in Him, the Eternal One.
The One who planned the great plan of redemption
and sent the Champion out of heaven long ago,
from the bosom of the Father down here below.

And He met the enemy in awful combat:
And arose victorious over death, hell, and the grave,
And ascended on High and led captivity captive.
The victory is in Him.

And if in Him you live and He lives in you,
   then the victory is on the inside.
Stir up the victory.
Shout the words in the face of the enemy:
"Victory!" "Victory!" "Victory!" — every day.
"Victory!" every night.
"Victory!" every moment.
For the Victorious One in me doth live.
Greater is He than all the forces of hell.
Greater is He than temptation
   and all that against me may come.
So I'll rest and rejoice every day.
For, you see, I am the victorious one.

DOUBT AND FEAR

Doubt and fear are the two tormenting twins
   of the enemy down here,
      sent to harrass and rob you of God's blessings.
But faith and love
   come from above.
Faith and love — for faith worketh by love.
And faith working by love
   will give you victory in every circumstance —
   will give you deliverance out of every problem.
Faith and love sent from heaven above.
Faith and love born of your spirit
   that is regenerated and born again:

The love of God shed abroad in your spirit.
Faith rising up out of the Word
    upon which you meditate and think.

So cast aside doubt and fear
    for they have no place in you
    as you walk down here.
For He has not given us the spirit of fear,
    but of power and of love and of a sound mind.
So cast away doubt and fear
    as you'd pull off your coat or cloak
    and throw it to one side.
And rise up and walk in love,
    and act in faith.
And all the heavenly blessings from above
    shall be at your disposal.
And in His great plan,
    you'll live and enjoy His blessings,
    as you walk in this clime.
And so you shall rejoice and be glad,
    for, you see, this is the day
    and this is the hour of your time.

These psalms came during Campmeeting, a public assembly, and they are in line with Colossians 3:16. Do you see how they both teach and admonish us? If you did not know what was contained in these psalms, they would teach you. If you already knew what was being spoken, they would admonish you.

There is also the speaking of psalms, hymns, and spiritual songs in the private prayer life as believers commune with God. Such speaking is especially in line with Ephesians 5:19 as we have already seen in Chapter 9.

"Well, how do you get there, Brother Hagin?" you may ask. "I've never spoken to myself in psalms, and hymns, and spiritual songs."

First, of course, you must be a born-again believer, having accepted Jesus as your Savior. Then, you must be baptized in the Holy Spirit with the Bible evidence of speaking in tongues.

As you begin to practice praying at length in other tongues, you will fine-tune your spirit to the Spirit of God. You see, psalms come out of your spirit where the Holy Ghost resides. He is not in your head, and your head has nothing to do with helping you "make up" psalms. Psalms are not of human invention, but come by the Holy Spirit's unction.

When you pray at length in the Spirit in other tongues, you will find that from the inside of you, from your spirit, a song or utterance will arise.

You may sing in tongues; then you may sing the interpretation. However, it is not always necessary to sing the interpretation. Just go ahead and sing in tongues, worshipping the Lord.

As you exercise yourself in these things, perhaps a word or phrase in a known tongue will rise up within you.

Step out in faith, and speak what you are given. If you will exercise faith in this area, it will enrich your life spiritually. You'll move up to another dimension, a higher level spiritually.

And when Spirit-filled believers will do this at home in personal communion with God, when they assemble together, the power of God will come into manifestation in a measure they have never seen.

God wants to bring us to the place where we will demonstrate glory to Him.

During the Monday night meeting of Campmeeting '87, just after I had shared what we have discussed in this chapter, we lifted our hands and worshipped God. And I heard the Spirit of God say, "It will take a little while for you to change. But after a little while, you will see the results. The power shall be manifested; the glory shall come to reside in your midst. It will not be manifested occasionally, but it will reside in your midst. And the glory of the Lord will be revealed unto thee and thou shalt be made a blessing unto many."

Chapter 11
True New Testament Worship

We must realize that the saints of the Old Testament weren't a *spiritual* house. Israel was called the "house" of Israel, and the word "house" was used in the Old Testament, but these people were spiritually dead people — they weren't born again. The Old Testament priests offered up only physical sacrifices. Therefore, they were not a "spiritual" house.

Under the New Covenant, in First Peter chapter 2, the Bible calls believers, "... *LIVELY stones ... built up a SPIRITUAL house....*"

> **1 PETER 2:5**
> 5 Ye also, as lively stones, are built up a spiritual house, an holy priesthood [the whole Body of Christ], **TO OFFER UP SPIRITUAL SACRIFICES,** acceptable to God by Jesus Christ.

This verse says that as a holy priesthood, we are "... *to offer up spiritual sacrifices....*" What are the spiritual sacrifices we are to offer up?

Our Bodies as a Living Sacrifice

> **ROMANS 12:1**
> 1 I beseech you therefore, brethren, by the mercies of God, that ye present your bodies a living sacrifice, holy, acceptable unto God, which is your reasonable service.

True New Testament worship includes the presenting of our bodies as a living sacrifice unto God. The Bible says *this* is the spiritual sacrifice acceptable to God as *a*

139

spiritual house and as *a holy priesthood:* "*Ye also, as lively stones, are built up a spiritual house, an holy priesthood, to offer up SPIRITUAL SACRIFICES, acceptable to God by Jesus Christ*" (1 Peter 2:5).

The *King James Version* of the Bible says we are to present our bodies as "a *living* sacrifice." Other translations say that we are to present our bodies as "*spiritual worship*" or as "a spiritual service of worship." The Bible calls this our reasonable service.

It is part of *true* spiritual worship for believers under the New Testament to offer our bodies unto God as a spiritual sacrifice. When the Church starts worshipping God according to His plan for New Testament worship — you talk about worship!

Jesus said to me in this visitation, "If the people aren't taught about spiritual worship, *true* New Testament worship, they won't get it. They do not know about true worship. They know a little bit about praising Me, but nothing about true worship."

The spiritual worship of presenting their bodies a living sacrifice, holy, acceptable unto God is something many Charismatics know nothing about.

I know because I've been around them. I can see why the Lord said, "Charismatics know a little about praising Me, but nothing about true worship." Because you can see some Charismatics running around talking in tongues, smoking cigarettes, and sipping cocktails! By such actions, they prove that they don't know a thing about *true spiritual worship!*

When people got over into the Charismatic Movement, they seemed to get free from *everything* — all laws, all discipline, all commitment, all restraints. But we can't let

our liberty be evil spoken of. God wants transfigured
bodies — bodies presented as "... *a living sacrifice, holy,
acceptable unto God, which is your reasonable service"*
(Rom. 12:1). It is your spiritual worship to present your
body unto God.

Let's see what else God wants as a part of *true* New
Testament spiritual worship:

> **ROMANS 12:2**
> 2 And be not conformed to this world: but be ye
> transformed by the renewing of your mind....

*God wants transfigured bodies and He wants trans-
formed minds.* These are the spiritual sacrifices the Bible
says the believer is to offer up to God.

Many people are trying to serve God with the same
old unrenewed mind they had before they were born again.
No wonder they're still having so much trouble with their
bodies and with their thoughts! It takes *work* and
discipline to renew your mind. It doesn't come by simply
attending church or by praying, and it doesn't come over-
night. It requires diligent meditation in God's Word, and
learning to change your ways and patterns of thinking to
line up with what His Word says. But renewing our minds
is *not an option* if we're going to be *true New Testament
worshippers.* A transformed mind is part of the spiritual
worship we are to offer up to God.

The Sacrifice of Praise

Hebrews 13:15 says we are to offer up to God the
sacrifice of praise which is the fruit of our lips, giving

thanks unto His Name! That is a sacrifice acceptable to God, and part of our *spiritual* worship. The fruit of our lips offering praise to God is part of *true* New Testament worship.

EPHESIANS 5:20
20 Giving thanks always for all things unto God and the Father in the name of our Lord Jesus Christ.

HEBREWS 13:15
15 By him [Jesus] therefore let us [What are we to do under the New Covenant?] offer the SACRIFICE of PRAISE to God continually, that is, the fruit of our lips giving thanks to his name.

What does the Bible mean by "the sacrifice of praise?" And how are we going to offer it to God? Look at this verse again: ". . . *let us offer the sacrifice of praise to God continually, that is, the fruit of our lips giving THANKS to his name.*"

Therefore, the Bible says New Testament praise is: ". . . *the fruit of our lips giving thanks to his name.*"

Let's see what the Bible has to say about the fruit of our lips.

PHILIPPIANS 3:1
1 Finally, my brethren, REJOICE in the Lord. . . .

PHILIPPIANS 4:4
4 REJOICE in the Lord alway: and again I say, Rejoice.

1 THESSALONIANS 5:16,18
16 REJOICE evermore. . . .

18 In every thing GIVE THANKS: for this is the will of God in Christ Jesus concerning you.

We can't thank God *for* the devil's work. That would be unscriptural. We aren't to *thank* God for what the devil is doing, but in the midst of it, we can give praise to God.

When I was just starting out in the ministry, I drove down the road many times preaching prosperity, knowing that it is right — that it is God's Word, but I was the most unlikely candidate for prosperity you ever saw. I drove an old worn-out car. In fact, I finally sold it for junk; I couldn't have sold it otherwise. I had a hole in one pocket and a dime and a pocketknife in the other pocket. But I would go down the highway praising and thanking God. Did I thank God *because* I didn't have any money? NO! I praised and thanked God because even in the midst of not having any money, His Word is true and I had another opportunity to believe Him and to prove that His Word works. I thanked God in the midst of what I was going through.

"Yeah, but you don't understand, Brother Hagin, they don't let me sing in the choir!"

Thank God.

"But they never call on me to do anything in church!"

Thank God. *If* you're *filled* with the Spirit, you *can* thank Him, and you *will thank Him!*

Now there is something more you need to see in the passage we examined in Chapter 9. This time, pay particular attention to the capitalized words.

EPHESIANS 5:18-20
18 ... BE FILLED WITH THE SPIRIT;
19 SPEAKING to yourselves in psalms and hymns and spiritual songs, SINGING and MAKING MELODY in your heart to the Lord;
20 GIVING THANKS ALWAYS for all things unto God and the Father in the name of our Lord Jesus Christ.

Remember that Jesus said, "The New Testament emphasizes the individual believer being filled with the Spirit, worshipping God in the Spirit." And He directed me to these verses.

Do you see that Ephesians 5:20 has to do with the offering up of the spiritual sacrifice of praise, the fruit of our lips giving thanks?

One filled with the Spirit will be full of thanksgiving — thanking God for His great plan of redemption He sent Jesus Christ to consummate; thanking Him for every good and perfect gift. True New Testament worship is to live a *life* of thanksgiving. What a difference giving thanks will make in you!

What is *God's plan* for the New Testament believer? To be filled with the Spirit, singing and making melody, and giving thanks always. That's true New Testament worship.

The New Testament puts emphasis on being filled with the Spirit, and on worshipping God *in the Spirit.* It doesn't say anything about clapping. I don't think you could clap in the Spirit; you can dance in the Spirit, and you can even laugh in the Spirit. Laughing in the Spirit will set you free!

Laughing in the Spirit

I was holding a meeting in a certain church, and the pastor of the church had been having all kinds of trouble. He told us later that he'd been bound with a spirit of heaviness for thirteen years. In this meeting, one of the RHEMA singers began laughing, and some of the rest of us began to laugh with him. This pastor told me later, "As I was watching the singers, I began to laugh in the natural just because they were laughing. Suddenly, I began to laugh in the Spirit, and I laughed and laughed and laughed. When I woke up the next morning, for the first time in thirteen years, that spirit of heaviness was gone, and I just started laughing again."

That's an example of what laughing in the Spirit did for one pastor. But don't just try to put on something. Whatever we do, it must be done *in the Spirit.*

If the anointing is not there, don't try to put something on because then it will be in the flesh. Yes, there is a laughter in the Spirit and there is a dance in the Spirit, but dancing or laughing in the Spirit would be the *results* of being *filled* with the Spirit. We must remember that the Bible does not specifically mention these. Yet, on the other hand, we know that the New Testament does say we are to rejoice in the Lord, to be *filled* with the Spirit, and to *move* in the Spirit. In order to be classified as true New Testament worship, whatever we do must be done *in the Spirit.*

In the New Testament, the emphasis of *true* worship is being filled with the Spirit, speaking to ourselves in psalms and hymns, giving thanks always, and presenting our bodies and transformed minds to God as a living sacrifice. God considers this our spiritual service. This is God's *plan for true worship.*

What is God's *purpose* in this plan? His purpose is to help us; to build us up! Since this is God's plan, we are to pursue *it* and follow *it!* Paul said, ". . . *forgetting those things which are behind, and reaching forth unto those things which are before, I press toward the mark for the prize of the high calling of God in Christ Jesus"* (Phil. 3:13,14).

There is a high calling for the Body of Christ. We stand on the threshold of a mighty move of God's Spirit. God has revealed His plan whereby we can enter into the fullness of His blessing. It is now up to us to pursue God's plan with God's purpose and usher in this next great outpouring.

But we must be willing to pay the price . . .

Chapter 12
Paying the Price

The following prayer of commitment came forth under the inspiration of the Holy Spirit during Homecoming '87 after I had taught on several of the subjects covered in this book. May each of us make this our ongoing prayer and may we choose to pay the price necessary to walk in God's plan — not only His plan for our individual lives, but His plan for the world in this hour.

Dear Father God, as Paul said, "I bow my knees unto the Father of our Lord Jesus Christ of whom the whole family in heaven and earth is named." We bow down before You.

Forgive us, Lord! We thought it was too great a price to pay and we weren't willing to pay that price.

We thought it was too great a price! But it's not! It's not! Forgive us! We've not entered into that, and we've not done all You said to do. Forgive us! Forgive us! You showed us those things and we thought, *They can't be. It can't be like that,* and we wouldn't pay that price. We thought, *It is too great a price; it is too big, too much to pay.*

May not a one of us — not a single one of us — hold back from what You are saying to us. Oh, Father God, though we don't always understand completely, may we dedicate and consecrate ourselves this day and this night to do Your will, so Your plan may be consummated in this hour — so that the work of God which must be done upon the earth shall be done. Oh, Father God, we dedicate ourselves and consecrate ourselves unto Your call, and unto Your bidding; not my plans, not our plans, but Your

147

plans. Father God, there is a move of the Spirit, and there is a work of the Spirit. There is a ministry *in* the Spirit and *of* the Spirit, and a demonstration of the power of God, and a manifestation of the Holy Ghost in this hour which You want manifested — that we've not been able to manifest because some of us have not been willing to pay the price. But we will pay it, Lord. We will, Lord. We will pay the price!

This will be a turning point in some of our lives, Lord. Oh, praise God! Amen. Some of us will look back to this night and say, "That was the place, and that was the hour, and that was the time." Oh, glory to God.

Some things are hard on the flesh, but, yes, we'll obey; we'll do it. Yes, Father. Yes! Oh, my, my, my! We get so entangled; we get Your plans entangled with our plans, and You can't bless us but just so far because they're our plans, and not Yours — they're our choices, and not Your choice. May we learn to listen to You.

Dear Father God, most of us know more than what we're living up to. Most of us know better than what we are living up to. Help us, dear Father God, so that we will respond to what You are saying unto our spirits. Life can be different; life *will* be different. Ministry can be different; ministry *will* be different.

Oh, there are many who will be turned completely around because they've been just partially walking in the light. They've been doing very little, but now then they will do much, and they will do more. Thank You for it.

Oh, my, my, my, the light will shine; the glory will come and it will be manifested. The cloud of God's glory, the cloud of His Presence shall overshadow thee. The very glory of God shall be shown, and we dedicate ourselves

unto it. We consecrate ourselves unto it in this hour, and
in this day. In the Name of Jesus. Praise God, hallelujah,
thank You, Lord.

May we not hold back in any measure from doing Your
will. May we not keep back part of the price. May we pay
the price to do Your will. May we not act anymore like
God really didn't mean what He said. *But He meant what
He said!* Oh, yes! And His way is best. His way is best.
And in the end, you'll not say, "It cost." You'll say, "It
paid! It paid! It paid rich dividends! It paid!"

But right at the moment, it seems sometimes like it
costs to completely follow God's will. And with some, it
may sometimes seem a terrible cost. Oh, yes, Father, but
our poor natural minds so many times get in our way and
hinder us. Yes, we'll not think that way — we'll not think
that it costs too much to obey God. We'll not touch that
in our thought life.

If the enemy brings a picture of it before our minds,
we'll just simply say, "Oh, Satan, that is just a picture.
I've turned that over to the Lord. He has it; He's working it out. It'll all work out just fine. And I'll be pleased
with whichever way it goes and whatever happens. I'll be
pleased." For Your way, Father, is best! And Your way
is right. Glory to God!

Yes, Lord, we rejoice in that. We will rejoice in that.
Yes, I realize that You're raising up many. Oh, my, they're
just in the beginning stages now. Yes, but if they will prove
faithful, if they will stay faithful, they will be promoted
and a stronger anointing will come upon them, and it will
be increased greatly. And they'll move into a higher place
of ministry, for there are different dimensions in the same
office. There are different measures — different dimensions

in the same office. And those who stay faithful will move up into a higher dimension of the same office. Yes, and a spirit of knowing will be manifested in a more perfect way in them.

And so they shall speak forth, and much good shall be accomplished. Yes, the plan of God shall be made known. We rejoice, and we are glad.

Pastors are so important in the plans and purposes of God, because the sheep must have a shepherd. And there are to be more pastors than any other ministry gift manifested. And they're so important in this hour. This is a crucial hour — a critical hour — we say a lot of times. But it is a very, very serious hour. And it is an hour for the pastor, the shepherd to be in full potential and manifestation of his office; to be in full manifestation and potential manifestation of his office. Oh, Father God, may pastors be endued with a new spirit. May every one of them be empowered with revelation gifts, a spirit of knowledge, and a spirit of knowing in their lives.

No, pastors will not stand, necessarily, in the office of the prophet. But they will be empowered with a spirit of knowing and especially with a spirit of wisdom, oh, Father God, until those things that have seemed a problem to them will be no more a problem, for they'll have the answer. They'll have the answer! And it will just seem that they have been standing on a ledge, so to speak, above the valley; but now they'll stand on the mountaintop. They'll stand on the mountaintop. And for some of them, their pulpit will no longer be a prison, but their pulpit will be a throne.

For Satan is a defeated foe. He'll not win in any situation, but he will lose every single time, for he is a defeated foe. And pastors shall have much cause for rejoicing.

Oh, my, my, my. And may a special unction rest upon those who go to foreign fields, Lord, where the darkness is so dark. May the light shine even more and may their lives be enhanced with Your glory.

And may every single one of us, whatever area of ministry we may be in, whatever area of life — oh, dear God, may every one of us be willing to pay the price, because there is a cost. Thank God, Jesus paid the price for our redemption and salvation. But there is a price to be paid when it comes to obeying You, and fulfilling the ministry that You called us to do. And sometimes, it means that we do not — that we even have to deny the flesh of legitimate pleasures and things that are all right, but we just have to spend that extra time, that extra time with You.

Oh, Father God, may not a single one of us forget this night or forget this day, but may every single one of us — from our very innermost being, say, "Lord, I'll pay the price no matter what others may do. I'll do Your work, Your will. Your plan shall be consummated in my life. Your will for my life and ministry shall be perfected. In the Name of Jesus."

Make this confession with me:

Dear Father God,

I am willing — I not only have a willing mind, but from my heart, my spirit — I have a willing spirit! I *will* to do YOUR will — to follow Your plan. Though it may be hard on the flesh, though there may be a cost, I'll pay the price and I'll do Your will. I'll follow Your plan. Your will shall be accomplished in my life, and Your plan shall be perfected in the Name of Jesus. I will not draw back. I will not go back on the words I've spoken here tonight no matter what it may seem to cost. No matter how much it may seem to hurt, I know the rewards are great and that it pays to obey God.

Thank You for working in my life. Thank You for preparing me for that which You have prepared for me. Thank You for showing me those things which I see not. Thank You for teaching me those things which I know not. Thank You for preparing me for that which You have prepared for ME. Your will, I will do. Hallelujah!

I purpose to be faithful, to be true, to be dedicated, to be consecrated — not just for tonight, not just in word but in action. And tomorrow and the next week and the next year and forever, I'm Yours! Use me, oh, Lord. Make me a blessing unto humanity.

May Your plan and purpose for my life and ministry be perfected in me. And it is God, God our Father, who is at work within me. Hallelujah. I yield to You. I trust in You, and I'll not allow my natural mind to dominate me. I'll maintain the vision. I'll maintain the glow. I'll maintain the commitment. And I'll not forget — with You, I will go.